MOTHER,
SISTER
AND
FOLLOWER

MOTHER, SISTER AND FOLLOWER

Mary the mother of Jesus
Mary of Bethany
Mary Magdalene

C. H. Spurgeon

CHRISTIAN
HERITAGE

Charles Haddon Spurgeon is considered the great Victorian preacher. He left a legacy for modern times that made him known as the 'Prince of Preachers'.

Look out for *Living by Revealed Truth* by Tom Nettles (ISBN 978-1-78191-122-8). He has spent more than fifteen years working on this magisterial biography of Charles Haddon Spurgeon which covers his life, ministry and also provides an indepth survey of his theology.

Copyright © Christian Focus Publications 2014

paperback ISBN 978-1-78191-405-2
epub ISBN 978-1-78191-447-2
Mobi ISBN 978-1-78191-450-2

Published in 2014
by
Christian Focus Publications, Ltd.
Geanies House, Fearn, Ross-shire,
IV20 1TW, Scotland, United Kingdom.
www.christianfocus.com

Cover design by Daniel van Straaten

Printed by
Bell and Bain, Glasgow

CONTENTS

About this book

This book contains six sermons preached by C. H. Spurgeon on the words or actions of three notable women called Mary. The first two sermons concern Mary the mother of Jesus, the next two examine the priorities of Mary of Bethany, and the final pair considers the witness of Mary Magdalene. As with all character studies, there is great scope in these selections for such a skilful preacher as Spurgeon to find much to commend for our imitation and to highlight as a challenge concerning the quality of our discipleship. Spurgeon believed he lived in difficult and dangerous days for the Christian church in Britain and his applications are therefore still very relevant for us in our time.

1

Mary's Song[1]

*And Mary said, 'My soul doth magnify the Lord,
and my spirit hath rejoiced in God my Saviour.'*
Luke 1:46, 47

Mary was on a visit when she expressed her joy in the language of this noble song. It were well if all our social intercourse were as useful to our hearts as this visit was to Mary. 'Iron sharpeneth iron; so a man sharpeneth the countenance of his friend.' Mary, full of faith, goes to see Elizabeth, who is also full of holy confidence, and the two are not long together

---

1. This sermon was preached on Sunday morning, December 25th, 1864, at the Metropolitan Tabernacle, Newington.

before their faith mounts to full assurance, and their full assurance bursts forth in a torrent of sacred praise. This praise aroused their slumbering powers, and instead of two ordinary village women, we see before us two prophetesses and poetesses, upon whom the Spirit of God abundantly rested. When we meet with our kinsfolk and acquaintance, let it be our prayer to God that our communion may be not only pleasant, but profitable; that we may not merely pass away time and spend a pleasant hour, but may advance a day's march nearer heaven, and acquire greater fitness for our eternal rest.

Observe, this morning, the sacred joy of Mary that you may imitate it. This is a season when all men expect us to be joyous. We compliment each other with the desire that we may have a 'Merry Christmas'. Some Christians who are a little squeamish do not like the word 'merry'. It is a right good old Saxon word, having the joy of childhood and the mirth of manhood in it; it brings before one's mind the old song of the waits, and the midnight peal of bells, the holly and the blazing log. I love it for its place in that most tender of all parables, where it is written, that, when the long-lost prodigal returned to his father safe and sound, 'They began to be merry.' This is the season when we are expected to be happy; and my heart's desire is, that in the highest and best sense, you who are believers may be 'merry'.

Mary's heart was merry within her; but here was the mark of her joy, it was all holy merriment, it was every drop of it sacred mirth. It was not such merriment as worldlings will revel in today and tomorrow, but such merriment as the angels have around the throne, where they sing, 'Glory to God in the highest,' while we sing 'On earth peace, goodwill towards men.' Such merry hearts have a continual feast. I want you, ye children of the bride-chamber, to possess today and tomorrow, yea, all your days, the high and consecrated bliss of Mary, that you may not only read her words, but use them for yourselves, ever experiencing their meaning: 'My soul doth magnify the Lord, and my spirit hath rejoiced in God my Saviour.'

Observe, first, that she sings; secondly, she sings sweetly; thirdly, shall she sing alone?

1. First observe, that *Mary Sings*. Her subject is a Saviour; she hails the incarnate God. The long-expected Messiah is about to appear. He for whom prophets and princes waited long, is now about to come, to be born of the virgin of Nazareth. Truly there was never a subject of sweeter song than this – the stooping down of Godhead to the feebleness of manhood. When God manifested his power in the works of his hands, the morning stars sang together, and the sons of God shouted for joy; but when God manifests himself, what music shall suffice for the grand psalm of adoring wonder? When wisdom and power are seen, these are but attributes; but in the incarnation it is the divine person which is revealed wrapt in a veil of our inferior clay: well might Mary sing, when earth and heaven even now are wondering at the condescending grace. Worthy of peerless music is the fact that 'the Word was made flesh and dwelt among us'. There is no longer a great gulf fixed between God and his people; the humanity of Christ has bridged it over.

We can no more think that God sits on high, indifferent to the wants and woes of men, for God has visited us and come down to the lowliness of our estate. No longer need we bemoan that we can never participate in the moral glory and purity of God, for if God in glory can come down to his sinful creature, it is certainly less difficult to bear that creature, bloodwashed and purified, up that starry way, that the redeemed one may sit down for ever on his throne. Let us dream no longer in sombre sadness that we cannot draw near to God so that he will really hear our prayer and pity our necessities, seeing that Jesus has become bone of our bone and flesh of our flesh, born a babe as we are born, living a man as we must live, bearing the same infirmities and sorrows, and bowing his head to the same death. O, can we not come with boldness by this new and living way, and have access to the throne of the heavenly grace, when Jesus meets us as Immanuel, God with us? Angels sang, they scarce knew why. Could they understand why God had become man? They must have known that herein was a mystery of condescension; but all the loving consequences which the incarnation involved even their acute minds could scarce have guessed; but we see the whole, and comprehend the grand design most fully. The manger of Bethlehem was big with glory; in the incarnation was wrapped up all the blessedness by which a soul, snatched from the depths of sin, is lifted up to the heights of glory. Shall not our clearer knowledge lead us to heights of song which angelic guesses could not reach? Shall the lips of cherubs move to flaming sonnets, and shall we who are redeemed by the blood of the incarnate God be treacherously and ungratefully silent!

> Did archangels sing thy coming?
> Did the shepherds learn their lays?
> Shame would cover me ungrateful,
> Should my tongues refuse to praise.

This, however, was not the full subject of her holy hymn. Her peculiar delight was not that there was a Saviour to be born, but that he was to be born of her. Blessed among women was she, and highly favoured of the Lord; but we can enjoy the same favour; nay, we must enjoy it, or the coming of a Saviour will be of no avail to us. Christ on Calvary, I know, takes away the sin of his people; but none have ever known the virtue of Christ upon the cross, unless they have the Lord Jesus formed in them as the hope of glory. The stress of the virgin's canticle is laid upon God's special grace to her. Those little words, the personal pronouns, tell us that it was truly a personal affair with her. 'My soul doth magnify the Lord, and my spirit hath rejoiced in God my Saviour.' The Saviour was peculiarly, and in an especial sense, hers. She sang no 'Christ for all', but 'Christ for me' was her glad subject.

Beloved, is Christ Jesus in your heart? Once you looked at him from a distance, and that look cured you of all spiritual diseases, but are you now living upon him, receiving him into your very vitals as your spiritual meat and drink? In holy fellowship you have oftentimes fed upon his flesh and been made to drink of his blood; you have been buried with him in baptism unto death; you have yielded yourselves a sacrifice to him and you have taken him to be a sacrifice for you; you can sing of him as the spouse did, 'His left hand is under my head, and his right hand doth embrace me... My beloved is mine, and I am his: he feedeth among the lilies.' This is a happy style of living, and all short of this poor slavish work, Oh! you can never know the joy of Mary unless Christ becomes truly and really yours; but oh! when he is yours, yours within, reigning in your heart, yours controlling all your passions, yours changing your nature, subduing your corruptions, inspiring you with hallowed emotions; yours within, a joy unspeakable and full of glory – oh! then you can sing, you must sing, who can restrain your tongue? If all the scoffers and mockers upon earth should bid you hold your peace, you must sing; for your spirit must rejoice in God your Saviour.

We should miss much instruction if we overlooked the fact that the choice poem before us is a hymn of faith. As yet there was no Saviour born, nor, as far we can judge had the virgin any evidence such as carnal sense requireth to make her believe that a Saviour would be born of her. 'How can this thing be?' was a question which might very naturally have suspended her song until it received an answer convincing to flesh and blood; but no such answer had been given. She knew that with God all things are possible, she had his promise delivered by an angel, and this was enough for her: on the strength of the Word which came forth from God, her heart leaped with pleasure and her tongue glorified his name. When I consider what it is which she believed, and how unhesitatingly she received the word, I am ready to give her, as a woman, a place almost as high as that which Abraham occupied as a man; and if I dare not call her the mother of the faithful, at least let her have due honour as one of the most excellent of the mothers in Israel. The benediction of Elizabeth, Mary right well deserved, 'Blessed is she that believeth.' To her the 'substance of things hoped for' was her faith, and that was also her 'evidence of things not seen'; she knew, by the revelation of God, that she was to bear the promised seed who should bruise the serpent's head; but other proof she had none.

This day there are these among us who have little or no conscious enjoyment of the Saviour's presence; they walk in darkness and see no light; they are groaning over inbred sin, and mourning because corruptions prevail; let them now trust in the Lord, and remember that if they believe on the Son of God, Christ Jesus is within them; and by faith they may right gloriously chant the hallelujah of adoring love. What though the sun gleam not forth today, the clouds and mists have not quenched his light; and though the Sun of Righteousness shine not on thee at this instant, yet he keeps his place in yonder skies, and knows no variableness, neither shadow of a turning. If with all thy digging, the well spring not up, yet there abideth a constant fullness in that deep, which croucheth beneath in the heart and purpose of a God of love. What, if like David, thou art much cast down, yet like him do thou say unto thy soul, 'Hope thou in God, for I shall yet praise him for the help of his countenance.' Be glad then with Mary's joy: it is the joy of a Saviour completely hers, but evidenced to be so, not by sense, but by faith. Faith has its music as well as Sense, but it is of a diviner sort: if the viands on the table make men sing and dance, feastings of a more refined and etherial nature can fill believers with a hallowed plenitude of delight.

Still listening to the favoured virgin's canticle, let me observe that her lowliness does not make her stay her song; nay, it imports a sweeter note into it. 'For he hath regarded the low estate of his handmaiden.' Beloved friend, you are feeling more intensely than ever the depth of your natural depravity, you are humbled under a sense of your many failings, you are so dead and earth-bound even in this house of prayer, that you cannot rise to God; you are heavy and sad, while our Christmas carols have been ringing in your ears; you feel yourself to be today so useless to the Church of God, so insignificant, so utterly unworthy, that your unbelief whispers, 'Surely, surely, you have nothing to sing for.' Come, my brother, come my sister, imitate this blessed virgin of Nazareth, and turn that very lowliness and meanness which you so painfully feel, into another reason for unceasing praise; daughters of Zion, sweetly say in your hymns of love, 'He hath regarded the low estate of his handmaiden.' The less worthy I am of his favours, the more sweetly will I sing of his grace. What if I be the most insignificant of all his chosen; then will I praise him who with eyes of love has sought me out, and set his love upon me. 'I thank thee, O Father, Lord of heaven and earth, that whilst thou hast hid these things from the wise and prudent, thou hast revealed them unto babes: even so, Father; for so it seemed good in thy sight.'

I am sure, dear friends, the remembrance that there is a Saviour, and that this Saviour is yours, must make you sing; and if you set side by side with it the thought that you were once sinful, unclean, vile, hateful, and an enemy to God, then your notes will take yet a loftier flight, and mount to the third heavens, to teach the golden harps the praise of God.

It is right well worthy of notice, that the greatness of the promised blessing did not give the sweet songstress an argument for suspending her thankful strain. When I meditate upon the great goodness of God in loving his people before the earth was, in laying down his life for us, in pleading our cause before the eternal throne, in providing a paradise of rest for us for ever, the black thought has troubled me, 'Surely this is too high a privilege for such an insect of a day as this poor creature, man.' Mary did not look at this matter unbelievingly; although she appreciated the greatness of the favour, she did but rejoice the more heartily on that account. 'For he that is mighty hath done to me great things.' Come, soul, it is a great thing to be a child of God, but thy God doeth great wonders, therefore be not staggered through unbelief, but triumph in thine adoption, great mercy though it be. Oh! it is a mighty mercy, higher than the mountains, to be chosen of God from all eternity, but it is true that even so are his redeemed chosen, and therefore sing thou of it. It is a deep and unspeakable blessing to be redeemed with the precious blood of Christ, but thou art so redeemed beyond all question. Therefore doubt not, but shout aloud for gladness of heart. It is a rapturous thought, that thou shalt dwell above, and wear the crown, and wave the palm branch for ever; let no mistrust interrupt the melody of thy psalm of expectation, but –

> Loud to the praise of love divine,
> Bid every string awake.

What a fullness of truth is there in these few words: 'He that is mighty hath done to me great things.' It is a text from which a glorified spirit in heaven might preach an endless sermon. I pray you, lay hold upon the thoughts which I have in this poor way suggested to you, and try to reach where Mary stood in holy exultation. The grace is great, but so is its giver; the love is infinite, but so is the heart from which it wells up; the blessedness is unspeakable, but so is the divine wisdom which planned it from of old. Let our hearts take up the Virgin's Magnificat, and praise the Lord right joyously at this hour.

Still further, for we have not exhausted the strain, the holiness of God has sometimes damped the ardour of the believer's joy; but not so in Mary's case. She exults in it; 'And holy is his name.' She weaves even that bright attribute into her song. Holy Lord! when I forget my Saviour, the thought of thy purity makes me shudder; standing where Moses stood upon the holy mountain of thy law, I do exceeding fear and quake. To me, conscious of my guilt, no thunder could be more dreadful than the seraph's hymn of 'Holy! holy! holy! Lord God of Sabaoth.' What is thy holiness but a consuming fire which must utterly destroy me – a sinner? If the heavens are not pure in thy sight and thou chargedst thine angels with folly, how much less then canst thou bear with vain, rebellious man, that is born of woman? How can man be pure, and how can thine eyes look upon him without consuming him quickly in thine anger? But, O thou Holy One of Israel, when my spirit can stand on Calvary and see thy holiness vindicate itself in the wounds of the man who was born at Bethlehem, then my spirit rejoices in that glorious holiness which was once her terror. Did the thrice holy God stoop down to man and take man's flesh? Then is there hope indeed! Did a holy God bear the sentence which his own law pronounced on man? Does that holy God incarnate now spread his wounded hands and plead for me? Then my soul, the holiness of God shall be a consolation to thee. Living waters from this sacred well I draw; and I will add to all my notes of joy this one, 'and holy is his name.' He hath sworn by his holiness, and he will not lie, he will keep his covenant with his anointed and his seed for ever.

When we take to ourselves the wings of eagles, and mount towards heaven in holy praise, the prospect widens beneath us; even so as Mary poises herself upon the poetic wing, she looks adown the long aisles of the past, and beholds the mighty acts of Jehovah in the ages long back. Mark how her strain gathers majesty; it is rather the sustained flight of the eagle-winged Ezekiel than the flutter of the timid dove of Nazareth. She sings, 'His mercy is on them that fear him from generation to generation.' She looks beyond the captivity, to the days of the kings, to Solomon, to David, along through the Judges into the wilderness, across the Red Sea to Jacob, to Isaac, to Abraham, and onward, till, pausing at the gate of Eden, she hears the sound of the promise, 'The seed of the woman shall bruise the serpent's head.' How magnificently she sums up the book of the wars of the Lord, and rehearses the triumphs of Jehovah, 'He hath showed strength with his arm; he hath scattered the proud in the imagination of their hearts.' How delightfully is mercy intermingled with judgment in the next canto of her psalm: 'He hath put down the mighty from their seats, and exalted them of low degree. He hath filled the hungry with good things; and the rich he hath sent empty away.'

My brethren and sisters, let us, too, sing of the past, glorious in faithfulness, fearful in judgment, teeming with wonders. Our own lives shall furnish us with a hymn of adoration. Let us speak of the things which we have made touching the King. We were hungry, and he filled us with good things; we crouched upon the dunghill with the beggar, and he has enthroned us among princes; we have been tossed with tempest, but with the Eternal Pilot at the helm, we have known no fear of shipwreck; we have been cast into the burning fiery furnace, but the presence of the Son of Man has quenched the violence of the flames.

Tell out, O ye daughters of music, the long tale of the mercy of the Lord to his people in the generations long departed. Many waters could not quench his love, neither could the floods drown it; persecution, famine, nakedness, peril, sword – none of these have separated the saints from the love of God which is in Christ our Lord. The saints beneath the wing of the Most High have been ever safe; when most molested by the enemy, they have dwelt in perfect peace: 'God is their refuge and strength, a very present help in trouble.' Ploughing at times the blood red wave, the ship of the Church has never swerved from her predestined path of progress. Every tempest has favoured her: the hurricane which sought her ruin has been made to bear her the more swiftly onward. Her flag has braved these eighteen hundred years the battle and the breeze, and she fears not what may yet be before her. But, lo! she nears the haven; the day is dawning when she shall bid farewell to storms; the waves already grow calm beneath her; the long-promised rest is near at hand; her Jesus himself meets her, walking upon the waters; she shall enter into her eternal haven, and all who are on board shall, with their Captain, sing of joy, and triumph, and victory through him who hath loved her and been her deliverer.

When Mary thus tuned her heart to glory in her God for his wonders in the past, she particularly dwelt upon the note of election. The highest note in the scale of my praise is reached when my soul sings, 'I love him because he first loved me.' Well does Kent put it:

> A monument of grace,
> A sinner saved by blood;
> The streams of love I trace,

Up to the fountain, GOD;
And in his mighty breast I see,
Eternal thoughts of love to me.

We can scarcely fly higher than the source of love in the mount of God. Mary has the doctrine of election in her song: 'He hath put down the mighty from their seats, and exalted them of low degree. He hath filled the hungry with good things; and the rich he hath sent empty away.' Here is distinguishing grace, discriminating regard; here are some suffered to perish; here are others, the least deserving and the most obscure, made the special objects of divine affection. Do not be afraid to dwell upon this high doctrine, beloved in the Lord. Let me assure you that when your mind is most heavy and depressed, you will find this to be a bottle of richest cordial. Those who doubt these doctrines, or who cast them into the cold shade, miss the richest clusters of Eshcol; they lose the wines on the lees well refined, the fat things full of marrow; but you who by reason of years have had your senses exercised to discern between good and evil, you know that there is no honey like this, no sweetness comparable to it. If the honey in Jonathan's wood, when but touched enlightened the eyes to see, this is honey that will enlighten your heart to love and learn the mysteries of the kingdom of God. Eat, and fear not a surfeit; live upon this choice dainty, and fear not that you shall grow weary of it, for the more you know, the more you will want to know; the more your soul is filled, the more you will desire to have your mind enlarged, that you may comprehend more and more the eternal, everlasting, discriminating love of God.

But one more remark upon this point. You perceive she does not finish her song till she has reached the covenant.

When you mount as high as election, tarry on its sister mount, the covenant of grace. In the last verse of her song, she sings, 'As he spake to our fathers, to Abraham, and to his seed for ever.' To her, that was the covenant; to us who have clearer light, the ancient covenant made in the council chamber of eternity, is the subject of the greatest delight. The covenant with Abraham was in its best sense only a minor copy of that gracious covenant made with Jesus, the everlasting Father of the faithful, ere the blue heavens were stretched abroad. Covenant engagements are the softest pillows for an aching head; covenant engagements with the surety, Christ Jesus, are the best props for a trembling spirit.

> His oath, his covenant, his blood,
> Support me in the raging flood;
> When every earthly prop gives way,
> This still is all my strength and stay.

If Christ did swear to bring me to glory, and if the Father swore that he would give me to the Son to be a part of the infinite reward for the travail of his soul; then, my soul, till God himself shall be unfaithful, till Christ shall cease to be the truth, till God's eternal council shall become a lie, and the red roll of his election shall be consumed with fire, thou art safe. Rest thou, then, in perfect peace, come what will; take thy harp from the willows, and never let thy fingers cease to sweep it to strains of richest harmony. O for grace from first to last to join the Virgin in her song.

2. Secondly, *She Sings Sweetly*. She praises her God right heartily. Observe how she plunges into the midst of the subject. There is no preface, but 'My soul doth magnify the Lord, and my spirit hath rejoiced in God my Saviour.'

When some people sing, they appear to be afraid of being heard. Our poet puts it:

> With all my powers of heart and tongue
> I'll praise my Maker in my song;
> Angels shall hear the notes I raise,
> Approve the song, and join the praise.

I am afraid angels frequently do not hear those poor, feeble, dying whisperings, which often drop from our lips merely by force of custom. Mary is all heart; evidently her soul is on fire; while she muses, the fire burns; then she speaks with her tongue. May we, too, call home our wandering thoughts, and wake up our slumbering powers to praise redeeming love. It is a noble word that she uses here: 'My soul doth magnify the Lord.' I suppose it means, 'My soul doth endeavour to make God great by praising him.' He is as great as he can be in his being; my goodness cannot extend to him; but yet my soul would make God greater in the thoughts of others, and greater in my own heart. I would give the train of his glory wider sweep; the light which he has given me I would reflect; I would make his enemies his friends; I would turn hard thoughts of God into thoughts of love. 'My soul would magnify the Lord.'

Old Trapp says, 'My soul would make greater room for him.' It is as if she wanted to get more of God into her, like Rutherford, when he says, 'Oh! that my heart were as big as heaven, that I might hold Christ in it;' and then he stops himself: 'But heaven and earth cannot contain him. Oh, that I had a heart as big as seven heavens, that I might hold the whole of Christ within it.' Truly this is a larger desire than we can ever hope to have gratified; yet still our lips shall sing, 'My soul doth magnify the Lord.' Oh! if I could

23

crown him; if I could lift him higher! If my burning at the stake would but add a spark more light to his glory, happy should I be to suffer. If my being crushed would lift Jesus an inch higher, happy were the destruction which should add to his glory! Such is the hearty spirit of Mary's song.

Again, her praise is very joyful: 'My spirit hath rejoiced in God my Saviour.' The word in the Greek is a remarkable one. I believe it is the same word which is used in the passage, 'Rejoice ye in that day and leap for joy.' We used to have an old word in English which described a certain exulting dance, 'a galliard.' That word is supposed to have come from the Greek word here used. It was a sort of leaping dance; the old commentators call it a *levalto*. Mary in effect declares, 'My spirit shall dance like David before the ark, shall leap, shall spring, shall bound, shall rejoice in God my Saviour.' When we praise God, it ought not to be with dolorous and doleful notes. Some of my brethren praise God always on the minor key, or in the deep, deep bass: they cannot feel holy till they have the horrors. Why cannot some men worship God except with a long face? I know them by their very walk as they come to worship: what a dreary pace it is! How solemnly proper and funereal indeed! They do not understand David's Psalm:

> Up to her courts with joys unknown,
> The sacred tribes repair.

No, they come up to their Father's house as if they were going to jail, and worship God on the Sunday as if it were the most doleful day in the week.

It is said of a certain Highlander, when the Highlanders were very pious, that he once went to Edinburgh, and when he came back again he said he had seen a dreadful sight on

Sabbath, he had seen people at Edinburgh going to kirk with happy faces. He thought it wicked to look happy on Sunday; and that same notion exists in the minds of certain good people hereabouts; they fancy that when the saints get together they should sit down, and have a little comfortable misery, and but little delight. In truth, moaning and pining is not the appointed way for worshipping God. We should take Mary as a pattern. All the year round I recommend her as an example to fainthearted and troubled ones. 'My spirit hath rejoiced in God my Saviour.' Cease from rejoicing in sensual things, and with sinful pleasures have no fellowship, for all such rejoicing is evil, but you cannot rejoice too much in the Lord.

I believe that the fault with our public worship is that we are too sober, too cold, too formal. I do not exactly admire the ravings of our Primitive-Methodist friends when they grow wild; but I should have no objection to hear a hearty 'Hallelujah!' now and then. An enthusiastic burst of exultation might warm our hearts; the shout of 'Glory!' might fire our spirits. This I know, I never feel more ready for true worship than when I am preaching in Wales, when the whole sermon throughout, the preacher is aided rather than interrupted by shouts of 'Glory to God!' and 'Bless his name!' Why then one's blood begins to glow, and one's soul is stirred up, and this is the true way of serving God with joy. 'Rejoice in the Lord alway; and again I say, Rejoice.' 'My spirit hath rejoiced in God my Saviour.'

She sings sweetly, in the third place, because she sings confidently. She does not pause while she questions herself, 'Have I any right to sing?' but no, 'My soul doth magnify the Lord, and my spirit hath rejoiced in God my Saviour. For he hath regarded the low estate of his handmaiden.' 'IF' is a sad enemy to all Christian happiness; 'but,' 'peradventure,' 'doubt,' 'surmise,' 'suspicion,' these are a race of highwaymen who waylay poor timid pilgrims and steal their spending money. Harps soon get out of tune, and when the wind blows from the doubting quarter, the strings snap by wholesale. If the angels of heaven could have a doubt, it would turn heaven into hell. 'If thou be the Son of God,' was the dastardly weapon wielded by the old enemy against our Lord in the wilderness. Our great foe knows well what weapon is the most dangerous. Christian, put up the shield of faith whenever thou seest that poisoned dagger about to be used against thee. I fear that some of you foster your doubts and fears. You might as well hatch young vipers, and foster the cockatrice. You think that it is a sign of grace to have doubts, whereas it is a sign of infirmity. It does not prove that you have no grace when you doubt God's promise, but it does prove that you want more; for if you had more grace, you would take God's Word as he gives it, and it would be said of you as of Abraham, that 'he staggered not at the promise of God, through unbelief, being fully persuaded that what he had promised he was able also to perform.'

God help you to shake off your doubts. Oh! these are devilish things. Is that too hard a word? I wish I could find a harder. These are felons; these are rebels, who seek to rob Christ of his glory; these are traitors who cast mire upon the escutcheon of my Lord. Oh! these are vile traitors; hang them on a gallows, high as Haman's; cast them to the earth, and let them rot like carrion, or bury them with the burial of an ass. Abhorred of God are doubts; abhorred of men let them be. They are cruel enemies to your souls, they injure your usefulness, they despoil you in every way. Smite them with the sword of the Lord and of Gideon! By faith in the promise seek to drive out these Canaanites and possess the land. O ye men of God, speak with confidence, and sing with sacred joy.

There is something more than confidence in her song. She sings with *great familiarity*, 'My soul doth magnify the Lord, and my spirit hath rejoiced in God my Saviour. For he that is mighty hath done to me great things; and holy is his name.' It is the song of one who draws very near to her God in loving intimacy.

I always have an idea when I listen to the reading of the Liturgy, that it is a slave's worship. I do not find fault with its words or sentences, perhaps of all human compositions, the Liturgical service of the Church of England is, with some exceptions, the noblest; but it is only fit for slaves, or at the best for subjects. The whole service through, one feels that there is a bound set round about the mountain, just as at Sinai. Its Litany is the wail of a sinner, and not the happy triumph of a saint. The service gendereth unto bondage, and has nothing in it of the confident spirit of adoption. It views the Lord afar off, as one to be feared rather than loved, and to be dreaded rather than delighted in. I have no doubt it suits those whose experience leads them to put the ten commandments near the communion table, for they hereby evidence that their dealings with God are still on the terms of servants and not of sons.

For my own part I want a form of worship in which I may draw near to my God, and come even to his feet, spreading my case before him, and ordering my cause with arguments; talking with him as a friend talketh with his friend, or a child with its father; otherwise the worship is little worth to me. Our Episcopalian friends, when they come here, are naturally struck with our service, as being irreverent, because it is so much more familiar and bold than theirs. Let us carefully guard against really deserving such a criticism, and then we need not fear it; for a renewed soul yearns after that very intercourse which the formalist calls irreverent. To talk with God as my Father, to deal with him as with one whose promises are true to me, and to whom I, a sinner washed in blood, and clothed in the perfect righteousness of Christ, may come with boldness, not standing afar off; I say this is a thing which the outer-court worshipper cannot understand. There are some of our hymns which speak of Christ with such familiarity that the cold critic says, 'I do not like such expressions, I could not sing them.' I quite agree with you, Sir Critic, that the language would not befit you, a stranger; but a child may say a thousand things which a servant must not. I remember a minister altering one of our hymns –

> Let those refuse to sing
> Who never knew our God;
> But favourites of the heavenly king
> May speak their joys abroad –

He gave it out – 'But *subjects* of the heavenly king.' Yes; and when he gave it out I thought, 'That is right; you are singing what you feel; you know nothing of discriminating grace' and special manifestations, and therefore you keep to your native level, 'Subjects of the heavenly king.' But oh, my heart wants a worship in which I can feel, and express the feeling that I am a favourite of the heavenly king, and therefore can sing his special love, his manifested favour, his sweet relationships, his mysterious union with my soul.

You never get it right till you ask the question, 'Lord, how is it that thou wilt manifest thyself unto us, and not unto the world?' There is a secret which is revealed to us, and not to the outside world; an understanding which the sheep receive and not the goats. I appeal to any of you who during the week are in an official position; a judge, for instance. You have a seat on the bench, and you wear no small dignity when you are there. When you get home there is a little fellow who has very little fear of your judgeship, but much love for your person, who climbs your knee, who kisses your cheek, and says a thousand things to you which are meet and right enough as they come from him, but which you would not tolerate in court from any man living. The parable needs no interpretation.

When I read some of the prayers of Martin Luther they shock me, but I argue with myself thus: 'It is true I cannot talk to God in the same way as Martin, but then perhaps Martin Luther felt and realized his adoption more than I do, and therefore was not less humble because he was more bold. It may be that he used expressions which would be out of place in the mouth of any man who had not known the Lord as he had done.' Oh my friends, sing this day of our Lord Jesus as one near to us. Get close to Christ, read his wounds, thrust your hand into his side, put your finger into the print of the nails, and then your song shall win a sacred softness and melody not to be gained elsewhere.

I must close by observing that while her song was all this, yet how very humble it was, and how full of gratitude. The Papist calls her, 'Mother of God,' but she never whispers such a thing in her song. No, it is 'God my Saviour'; just such words as the sinner who is speaking to you might use, and such expressions as you sinners who are hearing me can use too. She wants a Saviour, she feels it; her soul rejoices because there is a Saviour for her. She does not talk as though she could commend herself to him, but she hopes to stand accepted in the beloved. Let us then take care that our familiarity has always blended with it the lowliest prostration of spirit, when we remember that he is God over all, blessed for ever, and we are nothing but dust and ashes; he fills all things, and we are less than nothing and vanity.

The last thing was to be *Shall She Sing Alone?* Yes, she must, if the only music we can bring is that of carnal delights and worldly pleasures. There will be much music tomorrow which would not chime in with hers. There will be much mirth tomorrow, and much laughter, but I am afraid the most of it would not accord with Mary's song. It will not be, 'My soul doth magnify the Lord, and my spirit hath rejoiced in God my Saviour.' We would not stop the play of the animal spirits in young or old; we would not abate one jot of your relish of the mercies of God, so long 'as ye break not his command by wantonness, or drunkenness, or excess: but still, when you have had the most of this bodily exercise, it profiteth little, it is only the joy of the fleeting hour, and not the happiness of the spirit which abideth; and therefore Mary must sing alone, as far as you are concerned. The joy of the table is too low for Mary; the joy of the feast and the family grovels when compared with hers.

But shall she sing alone? Certainly not, if this day any of us by simple trust in Jesus can take Christ to be our own. Does the Spirit of God this day lead thee to say, 'I trust my soul on Jesus?' My dear friend, then thou hast conceived Christ: after the mystical and best sense of that word, Christ Jesus is conceived in thy soul. Dost thou understand him as the sin-bearer, taking away transgression? Canst thou see him bleeding as the substitute for men? Dost thou accept him as such? Does thy faith put all her dependence upon what he did, upon what he is, upon what he does? Then Christ is conceived in thee, and thou mayest go thy way with all the joy that Mary knew; and I was half ready to say, with something more; for the natural conception of the Saviour's holy body was not one-tenth so meet a theme for congratulation as the spiritual conception of the holy Jesus within your heart when he shall be in you the hope of glory.

My dear friend, if Christ be thine, there is no song on earth too high, too holy for thee to sing; nay, there is no song which thrills from angelic lips, no note which thrills an Archangel's tongue in which thou mayest not join. Even this day, the holiest, the happiest, the most glorious of words, and thoughts, and emotions belong to thee. Use them! God help thee to enjoy them; and his be the praise, while thine is the comfort evermore. Amen.

2

Obeying Christ's Orders[1]

*His mother saith unto the servants, Whatsoever he
saith unto you, do it.*
John 2:5

I t does not need a strong imagination to picture Mary,
probably at that time the widowed mother of our Lord.
She is full of love, and of a naturally kind, sympathetic
disposition. She is at a marriage; and she is very pleased that
her Son is there, with the first handful of his disciples. Their
being there has made a greater demand upon the provisions
than was expected, and the supply is running short; so she,

---

1.   Preached on Thursday evening, June 13th, 1889, at the Metropolitan Tabernacle, Newington.

with an anxiety that was natural to such a mother, of her years, and of her gentle spirit, thinks that she will speak to her Son, and tell him that there is a want, so she says to him, 'They have no wine.'

There was not much amiss in that, surely; but our Lord, who seeth not as man seeth, perceived that she was putting to the front her motherly relationship, at a time when it was needful that it should be in the background. How needful it was, history has shown; for the apostate church of Rome has actually made Mary a mediatrix, and prayers have been addressed to her; she has even been asked to use her maternal authority with her Son. It was well that our Saviour should check anything that might tend to give any countenance to Mariolatry, which has been altogether so mischievous; and it was needful for him to speak to his mother with somewhat more of sharpness than, perhaps, her conduct, in itself alone, might have required. So her august Son felt bound to say to her, 'Woman, what have I to do with thee in such a matter as this? I am not thy son as a miracle-worker; I cannot work to please thee. No; if I work a miracle as the Son of God, it cannot be as your son; it must be in another character. What have I to do with thee in this matter?' And he gives his reason: 'Mine hour is not yet come.'

It was a gentle rebuke, absolutely needful from the prescience of all that would follow. You can easily picture how Mary took it. She knew Christ's gentleness, his infinite love, how for thirty years there had never come anything from him that had grieved her spirit. So she drank in the reproof, and gently shrank back, thinking much more than she said; for she was always a woman who laid up these things, and pondered them in her heart. She says very little, but she thinks a great deal; and we see in her after conduct, in respect to this very miracle, that she thought very much of what Jesus had said to her. Brethren, you and I, with the very best intentions, may sometimes err towards our Lord; and if he then in any way rebukes us, and puts us back, if he disappoints our hope, if he does not allow our ambitious designs to prosper, let us take it from him as Mary took it from Jesus. Let us just feel that it must be right, and let us in silence possess ourselves in his presence.

Notice, then, this holy woman's quietude, ceasing to say a word, quietly drinking it all in; and then observe her wise admonition to the servants who were there to wait at the feast. Inasmuch as she had run before him, she would have them to follow after him, and she very wisely and kindly says to them, 'Whatsoever he saith unto you, do it. Do not go to him with any of your remarks. Do not try to press him forward; do not urge him on; he knows better than we do. Stand back, and wait till he speaks; and then be quick to obey every single word that he utters.'

Beloved, I wish that, when we have learned a lesson, we would try to teach it. Sometimes our Master gives us a sharp word all to ourselves, and we would not tell anybody else what he has said. In our private communions, he has spoken to our conscience and to our heart; and we need not go and repeat that, as Mary did not. But, having learned the lesson well, let us then say to our next friend, 'Do not err as I have done. Avoid the rock on which I struck just now. I fear that I grieved my Lord. My sister, I would not have you grieve him; my brother, I would try to tell you just what to do that you may please him in all things.' Do you not think that we should minister to mutual edification if we did that? Instead of telling the faults of others, let us extract the essence from the discoveries which we make of our own errors, and then administer that as a helpful medicine to those who are round about us.

This holy woman must have spoken with a good deal of power. Her tone must have been peculiarly forcible, and her manner must have made a great impression upon the servants, for you notice that they did exactly what she told them. It is not every servant who will let a guest come into the house, and set up to be mistress; but so it was when she spoke to those servants, with her deep, earnest tones, as a woman who had learned something that she could not tell, but who yet, out of that experience, had extracted a lesson for others. She must have spoken with a wonderful melting force when she said to them, 'Whatsoever he saith unto you, do it;' and they were all looking on with awe after she had spoken, drinking in her message to them as she had drunk in the message of the Lord.

Now I want tonight just to try to teach that lesson to myself and to you. I think that our own experience goes to show us that our highest wisdom, our very best prosperity, will lie in our cautiously keeping behind Christ, and never running before him, never forcing his hand, never tempting him, as they did who tempted God in the wilderness, prescribing to him to do this or that; but, in holy, humble obedience, taking these words as our life motto henceforth, 'Whatsoever he saith unto you, do it'. I will handle my text in this way: First, What? Secondly, Why? Thirdly, What then?

I. What is it that we are here bidden to do? In a word, it is to obey. You who belong to Christ, and are his disciples, take heed to this word of exhortation, 'Whatsoever he saith unto you, do it.'

I want you to notice, first of all, that these words were spoken, not to the disciples of Christ, but to the servants who, in the Greek, are here called *diakonois*, the persons who were brought in to wait at the table, and to serve the guests. I know not whether they were paid servants, or whether they were friends who kindly volunteered their services; but they were the waiters at the feast. They were not told to leave their master; they were not bidden to give up their avocation as waiters. They were servants, and they were to continue as servants; but still, for all that, they were to acknowledge Christ as their Master without casting off their obedience to the governor of the feast. Mary does not say to these people, 'Put down those pots, leave off carrying those dishes.' But while they continue to do what they were doing, she says to them, 'Whatsoever he saith unto you, do it.' I thought that point was well worthy of our notice, that these servants, still abiding as they were, yet were to render obedience to Christ.

That obedience, in the first place, would be *prepared* obedience. Mary came to get their minds ready to do what Christ should bid them. No man will obey Christ on a sudden, and keep on doing so. There must be a weighing, a considering; there must be a thoughtful, careful knowledge of what his will is, and a preparedness of heart, that whatever that will may be, as it is known so it shall be done. At first these servants did nothing. The guests wanted wine, but the servants did not go to Jesus, and say, 'Master, wine is needed.' Nay; but they stopped until he bade them fill the waterpots with water; then they filled them to the brim; but they did nothing till he bade them. A great part of obedience lies in not doing. I believe that, in the anxiety of many a trembling heart, the very best faith will be seen in not doing anything. When you do not know what to do, do nothing; and doing nothing, my brethren, will be found to be sometimes the very hardest work of all. In the case of a man in business, who has come into a difficulty, or of a sister with a sick child, or a sick husband, you know the impulse is to do something or other. If not the first thing that comes to hand, yet we feel that we must do something; and many a person has aggravated his sorrow by doing something, when, if he had bravely let it alone, believingly left it in God's hand, it would have been infinitely better for him.

'Whatsoever he saith unto you, do it.' But do not do what every whim or fancy in your poor brain urges you to do. Do not run before you are sent. They who run before God's cloud, will have to come back again; and very happy they will be if they find the way back again. Where Scripture is silent, be you silent. If there is no command thou hadst better wait till thou canst find some guidance. Blunder not on with a headlong anxiety, lost thou tumble into the ditch. 'Whatsoever he saith unto you,' do that; but until he speaks, sit thou still. My soul, be patient before God, and wait until thou knowest his bidding!

This prepared obedience was to be the obedience of the spirit, for obedience lies mainly there. True obedience is not always seen in what we do, or do not do; but it is manifest in the perfect submission to the will of God, and the strong resolve that saturates the spirit through and through, that what he bids us we will do.

Let your obedience, in the next place, be *perfect obedience*. 'Whatsoever he saith unto you, do it.' It is disobedience, and not obedience, which prompts us to select from the commands of Christ such as we care to obey. If thou sayest,

'I will do what Christ bids me as far as I choose,' thou hast in fact said, 'I will not do what Christ bids me, but I will do what I please to do.' That obedience is not true which is not universal. Imagine a soldier in the army, who, instead of obeying every command of his captain, omits this and that, and says that he cannot help it, or that he even means to omit certain things. Beloved, take heed of throwing any precept of thy Lord upon the dunghill. Every word that he has spoken to thee is more precious than a diamond. Prize it; store it up; wear it; let it be thy ornament and thy beauty.

'Whatsoever he saith unto you, do it,' whether it relates to the Church of God and its ordinances, or to your walk out of doors among your fellow men, or to your relationship in the family, or to your own private service for the Lord. 'Whatsoever.' See, there are to be no trimmings here, no cutting off of certain things: 'Whatsoever he saith unto you, do it.' Breathe this prayer at the present moment, 'Lord, help me to do whatsoever thou hast said! May I have no choice; may I never let my own will come in to interfere; but, if thou hast bidden me do anything, enable me to do it, whatever it may be!'

This obedience, then, being prepared and perfect, is to be also *practical* obedience: 'Whatsoever he saith unto you, do it.' Do not think about it, especially for a very long time, and then wait until it is more impressed upon you, or till there is a convenient season: 'Whatsoever he saith unto you, do it.' One of the great evils of the times is that of deliberating about a plain command of Christ, and asking, 'What will be the result of it?' What have you to do with results? 'But if I follow Christ in all things, I may lose my position.' What have you to do with that? When a soldier is bidden to go up to the cannon's mouth, he is very likely to lose his 'position' and something else; but he is bound to do it. 'Oh, but I might lose my opportunities of usefulness!' What do you mean? That you are going to do evil that good may come? That is what it comes to. Will you really, before God, look that matter in the face? 'Whatsoever he saith unto you, do it.' At any expense, at any risk, do it.

I have heard some say, 'Well, I do not like doing things in a hurry.' Very well, but what saith David? 'I made haste, and delayed not – to keep thy commandments.' Remember that we sin every moment that we delay to do anything commanded by Christ. Whether every moment of delay is a fresh sin, I cannot say; but if we neglect any command of his, we are living in a condition of perpetual sinning against him; and that is not a desirable position for any of Christ's disciples to live in. Beloved, 'whatsoever he saith unto you, do it.' Do not argue against it, and try to find some reason for getting off it.

I have known some believers who have not liked to have certain passages of Scripture read at the family altar, because they have rather troubled their consciences. If there is anything in the Bible that quarrels with you, you are wrong; the Bible is not. Come you to terms with it at once, and the only terms will be obey, obey, obey your Lord's will. I am not holding this up to you as a way of salvation; you know I should never think of doing that. I am speaking to those of you who are saved. You are Christ's servants, his saved ones; and now you have come to the holy discipline of his house, and this is the rule of it, 'Whatsoever he saith unto you, do it.'

Do it practically. Have we not been talking too much about what should be done by our friends, or observing what others do not do? Oh, that the Spirit of God would come upon us, that our own walk might be close with God, our own obedience be precise and exact, our own love to Christ be proved by our continual following in his steps! Ours should be practical obedience.

It must be also *personal* obedience: 'Whatsoever he saith unto *you*, do it.' You know how much there is done by proxy nowadays. Charity is done so. A is in a great deal of need, B hears of it, and is very sorry indeed, and so he asks C to come and help him; and then he goes to bed, and feels that he has done a good thing. Or else, when A has told his story to B, B looks out to see if there is some Society that will help him, although he never subscribes to the Society, because he does not think of doing that. His part is just to pass A on to C, or to the Society: and, having done that, he feels satisfied. Do you wish the Saviour to say, in the last great day, 'I was an hungred, and ye sent me to somebody else,' or, 'I was thirsty, and you directed me to the parish pump for drink'? Nothing of the kind. We must do something personally for Christ. So is it in the matter of endeavouring to win souls to Christ.

There is nothing like personally speaking to people, button-holing them, looking them in the eye, talking your own personal experience over with them, and pleading with them to fly to Christ for refuge. Personal obedience is what is wanted. If one of these persons who were waiting had said, when the command had come from Christ to fill the waterpots, 'John, you go and do that; William, you go and do that,' he would not have followed out Mary's command, 'Whatsoever he saith unto you, do it.' Do I touch the conscience of anybody here? Well, if so, from this time forth cease to be a servant of God by proxy, lest thou be saved by proxy, and to be saved by proxy will be to be lost. But do thou trust Christ for thyself, and then serve him for thyself, by his own mighty grace: 'Whatsoever he saith unto you, do it.'

It must also be *prompt* obedience. Do it at once; delay will take the bloom from the obedience. 'Whatsoever he saith unto you,' stand ready to obey. The moment that the command 'March' is given to the soldier, he marches. The moment a command comes to your heart, and you see it to be really in the Word of God, do it. Oh, the murdered resolutions that lie round about most men's lives! What they would have done, what they could have done, if they had but done it; but they have been building castles in the air, imagining lives they would like to lead, and not actually doing Christ's commands. Oh, for a prompt, personal, practical service to the Lord Jesus Christ!

And in our case it is to be *perpetual* obedience. Mary said to these waiters, 'Whatsoever he saith unto you, do it.' 'Keep on doing it; not only the first thing he says, but whatsoever he saith unto you. As long as this feast lasts, and he is here, do what my Son commands you.' So, beloved, as long as we are in this world, until life's latest hour, may the Holy Ghost enable us to do just what Jesus bids us do! Can you say, my brethren and sisters,

> Jesus, I my cross have taken,
> All to leave, and follow thee?

Is it your wish that, until you enter into his rest, you should always bear his yoke, and follow his footsteps? Temporary Christians are not Christians. Those who ask for furlough from this divine service have never entered it. We have put on our regimentals never to take them off. As certain old knights in times of war slept in their armour, and had the lance and shield always ready to hand, so must the Christian be from this time forth and for ever. 'Ours not to reason why,' ours not to delay when the command comes; but ours, while there is breath in our body, and life in our spirit, to serve him who hath redeemed us with his precious blood.

Thus I have feebly set before you what it is that we are called to do, that is, to obey Christ's orders.

2. Now for a few minutes let us ask, *Why is this to be done?* Beloved, why were these men to do what Jesus bade them? Let that melt into, 'Why are you and I to do what Jesus bids us?'

First, *Christ is by nature worthy of obedience.* I count it an honour to serve Christ. Oh, what is he? Perfect Man, rising nobly above us all; perfect God, infinitely majestic in his two natures. Why, it seems to me as if we ought to love to do his bidding, and long to be conformed to his image! Here is the rest for our aspiring spirit. Here are the glory and the honour and the immortality for which we pant. By the glory of Christ, whom you unseen adore, 'Whatsoever he saith unto you, do it.'

Beside that, *Christ is our only hope.* All our prospects for the future depend upon him. Glory be to his blessed name! There is none like him. If he were gone from us, and we could not trust in him, life would be an endless darkness, an abyss of woe. By all the glory of his nature, and all that we owe to him, and all that we look for from him, I charge you, beloved friends, 'Whatsoever he saith unto you, do it.'

More than that, *he is all-wise, and so fit to lead.* Who but he could get these people out of their trouble at the feast when they wanted wine? He knew the way out of it all, a way that would manifest his own glory, and make his disciples believe in him, and make everybody round about happy. But if he did not show the way, nobody could. So let us obey him, for his commands are so wise. He never has made a mistake, and he never will. Let us commit our way unto his keeping; and whatsoever he saith unto us, let us do it.

Besides, beloved, *Christ has hitherto rewarded our obedience.* Did you ever act rightly, and after all find it a mistake? Some of us have had to do very grievous things in our time that have gone sorely against the grain. Would we do them again? Ay, that we would, if they cost ten times as much! No man has ever, in looking back, to regret that he followed the voice of conscience and the dictates of God's Word; and he never will, though he should even go to prison and to death for Christ's sake. You may lose for Christ, but you shall never lose by Christ. When all comes to be totalled up, you shall be a greater gainer because of the apparent loss. He has never deceived you, and never misled you. Obedience to him has always brought you real solid peace. Therefore, 'whatsoever he saith unto you, do it.'

Yet once more, *Christ is our Master, and we must obey him.* I hope, beloved, that there is no one among us here who would call him Master, and yet not do the things that he says. We do not talk about him as one who was once great, but who is gone away, and whose influence is now upon the wane, because he is not up to 'the spirit of the age'. No, but he still lives, and we still commune with him. He is our Master and Lord. When we were baptized into his death, it was no mere matter of form; but we were dead to the world, and we lived to him. When we took his sacred name upon us, and were called Christians, it was no sham; we meant that he should be Captain, King, and Master of our spirits. He is no Baali, that is, domineering lord; but he is Ishi, our Man, our Husband; and, in his husbandly relationship he is Lord and Governor of every thought and every motion of our nature. Jesus, Jesus, thy yoke is easy, and thy burden is light! It is lightsome and joyous to bear it. To get away from it, would be misery indeed; and that is one reason why I say to you tonight, 'Whatsoever he saith unto you, do it,' because if you do not, you cast off your allegiance to him; and what are you going to do then? To whom will you go if you turn away from him? Every man must have a master. Will you be your own master? You cannot have a greater tyrant. Will you let the world be your master? Are you going to be a servant of 'society'? There are no worse slaves than these. Are you going to live for self, for honour, for what is called 'pleasure'? Ah, me, you may as well go down to Egypt, to the iron furnace, at once! To whom can we go? Jesus, to whom can we go, if we go away from thee? Thou hast the words of eternal life.

'Bind the sacrifice with cords, even unto the horns of the altar.' Throw another bond of love about me, another cord of sweet constraint, and let me never even think of parting with thee. Let me be crucified to the world, and the world to me. Do not your hearts pray after that fashion? Oh, to be wholly Christ's, entirely Christ's, for ever Christ's! Yes, yes, we will listen to the command, 'Whatsoever he saith unto you, do it.' I have given you the reason why we should obey Christ's orders.

3. And now, beloved, let me occupy the last few minutes in answering this question, *What will follow from this obedience?* Suppose we do whatever Christ commands us, what then? I will tell you what then.

The first thing is, that *you will feel free from responsibility*. The servant, who has done what his master has bidden him, may in his own mind fear that some dreadful consequences may follow, but he says to himself, 'It will be no fault of mine. I did what I was bidden to do.' Now, beloved, if you want to get rid of the whole burden of life, by faith do whatsoever Christ commands you. Then, if the heavens should seem about to fall, it would be no business of yours to shore them up. You have not to mend God's work, and keep it right. I remember what Mr John Wesley said to his preachers: 'Now, brethren, I do not want you to mend my rules. I want you to obey them.' That is pretty strong from John Wesley; but from our Lord Jesus Christ it comes most suitably. He does not want us to get altering, and mending, and touching up, and looking at consequences. No; do exactly what he tells you, and you have nothing to do with the consequences. You may have to bear them, but that he will give you grace to do; and it shall be your joy to bear all ill consequences that come of firm obedience to Christ.

This kind of doctrine does not suit the year 1889. If you go over to Scotland, and see where the Covenanters' graves are, anybody who thinks according to the spirit of this age will say that they were just a set of fools to have been so stubborn and so strict about doctrine as to die for it. Why, really, there is not anything in the new philosophy that is worth dying for! I wonder whether there is any 'modern thought' doctrine that would be worth the purchase of a cat's life. According to the teaching of the broad school, what is supposed to be true today may not be true tomorrow, so it is not worth dying for. We may as well put off the dying till the thing is altered; and if we wait a month, it will be altered, and thus, at the last, you may get the old creed back again. The Lord send it, and send us yet a race of men who will obey what he bids them, and do what he tells them, and believe what he teaches them, and lay their own wills down in complete obedience to their Lord and Master! Such a people will feel free from responsibility.

Then you *shall feel a sweet flow of love to Christ.* The disobedient child – well, he will not be turned out of the house, because he will not do the bidding of his mother and father; but when he does not submit to the rule of the house, he has a hard time of it, and he ought to have. There is that evening kiss, it is not as warm as it would have been; and that morning greeting, after long disobedience, has no happiness in it; and, indeed, the more kind father and mother are, the more unhappy he is. And the sweet love of Christ is such that it makes us unhappy in disobedience. You cannot walk contrary to Christ, and yet enjoy fellowship with him; and the more dear and near he would be to you, so much the wider does the gap seem to be when you are not doing his bidding.

Besides, there is no carrying out your faith except by doing as he bids you. That faith which lies only in a creed, or in a little pious book, is not good for much. Faith does what Christ bids it do, and it delights to do so. It rejoices to run risks, it delights to put off from the land, and get out to sea. It is glad to sacrifice itself when Jesus calls for it, because faith cannot be satisfied without bearing fruit, and the fruit of faith is obedience to him in whom we believe.

Beloved, I also think that, if we will obey Christ in what he says, *we shall be learning to be leaders.* Wellington used to say that no man is fit to command until he has learned to obey; and I am sure that it is so. We shall never see a race of really first-rate men unless our boys and girls are made to obey their parents in their childhood. The essential glory of manhood is lost when disobedience is tolerated; and, certainly, in the Church of God, the Lord does put his leading servants through very severe ordeals. The best place for the books of a minister is not his library, but a sick-bed very often. Affliction is our school; and before we can deal with others, God must deal with us. If thou wilt not obey, thou shalt not be set to command.

And lastly, I do believe that learning to obey is *one of the preparatives for the enjoyments of heaven.* Why, in heaven, they have no will but God's will! Their will is to serve him, and delight themselves in him; and if you and I do not learn here below what obedience to God is, and practice it, and carry it out, how could we hope to be happy in the midst of obedient spirits? Dear hearers, if you had never learned to trust Christ and obey him, how could you go to heaven? You would be so unhappy there that you would ask God to let you run into hell for shelter, for nothing would strike you with more horror than to be in the midst of perfectly holy people who find their delight in the service of God. May the Lord bring us to this complete obedience to Christ! Then this world will be an inclined plane, or a ladder such as Jacob saw, up which we shall trip with holy gladness till we come to the top, and find our heaven in perfect obedience to God.

It is not Mary who speaks to you tonight, but it is the Church of God, the mother of all who truly love Christ; and she says to you, 'Whatsoever he saith unto you, do it,' and if you will do it, he will turn the water into wine for you. He will make your love more glad and happy than it ever would have been without obeying him, and he will provide for you. Obey him, and he will comfort you. Obey him, and he will perfect you. Be with him in the ways of duty, and you shall be with him in the home of glory.

The Lord grant this, of his infinite grace, giving to us to know the will of Christ, and then working in us to will and to do of his own good pleasure! Amen and Amen.

3

Martha and Mary[1]

*Now it came to pass, as they went, that he entered into
a certain village: and a certain woman named Martha
received him into her house. And she had a sister called
Mary, which also sat at Jesus' feet, and heard his word.
But Martha was cumbered about much serving, and
came to him, and said, 'Lord, dost thou not care that my
sister hath left me to serve alone? Bid her therefore that she
help me.' And Jesus answered and said unto her, 'Martha, Martha, thou art careful and troubled about many
things: but one thing is needful: and Mary hath chosen
that good part, which shall not be taken away from her'.*
Luke 10:38-42

I t is not an easy thing to maintain the balance of our
spiritual life. No man can be spiritually healthy who
does not meditate and commune; no man, on the other
hand, is as he should be unless he is active and diligent
in holy service. David sweetly sang, 'He maketh me to lie
down in green pastures' – there was the contemplative; 'he
leadeth me beside the still waters' – there was the active

---

1.   This sermon was preached on Sunday morning, 24 April 1870, at
the Metropolitan Tabernacle, Newington.

and progressive; the difficulty is to maintain the two, and to keep each in its relative proportion to the other. We must not be so active as to neglect communion, nor so contemplative as to become unpractical.

In the chapter from which our text is taken, we have several lessons on this subject. The seventy disciples returned from their preaching tour flushed with the joy of success; and our Saviour, to refine that joy, and prevent its degenerating into pride, bids them rather rejoice that their names were written in heaven. He conducted their contemplations to the glorious doctrine of election, that grateful thoughts might sober them after successful work. He bids them consider themselves as debtors to the grace which reveals unto babes the mysteries of God, for he would not allow their new position as workers to make them forget that they were the chosen of God, and therefore debtors.

Our wise Master next returns to the subject of service, and instructs them by the memorable parable of the good Samaritan and the wounded man; and then as if they might vainly imagine philanthropy, as it is the service of Christ, to be the only service of Christ, and to be the only thing worth living for, he brings in the two sisters of Bethany; the Holy Ghost meaning thereby to teach us that while we ought to abound in service, and to do good abundantly to our fellow men, yet we must not fail in worship, in spiritual reverence, in meek discipleship, and quiet contemplation. While we are practical, like the seventy; practical, like the Samaritan; practical, like Martha; we are, also, like the Saviour, to rejoice in spirit, and say, 'Father, I thank thee,' and we are also like Mary, to sit down in quietude and nourish our souls with divine truth.

This short narrative I suppose might be paraphrased something after this fashion. Martha and Mary were two most excellent sisters, both converted, both lovers of Jesus, both loved by Jesus, for we are expressly told that he loved Mary and Martha and Lazarus. They were both women of a choice spirit, our Saviour's selection of their house as a frequent resort proved that they were an unusually gracious family. They are persons representative of different forms of excellence, and I think it altogether wrong to treat Martha as some have done, as if she had no love for good things, and was nothing better than a mere worldling. It was not so. Martha was a most estimable and earnest woman, a true believer, and an ardent follower of Jesus, whose joy it was to entertain Jesus at the house of which she was the mistress.

When our Lord made his appearance on this occasion at Bethany, the first thought of Martha was, 'Here is our most noble guest, we must prepare for him a sumptuous entertainment.' Perhaps she marked our Saviour's weariness, or saw some traces of that exhaustion which made him look so much older than he was, and she therefore set to work with the utmost diligence to prepare a festival for him; she was careful about many things, and as she went on with her preparations, fresh matters occurred to ruffle her mind, and she became worried; and, being somewhat vexed that her sister took matters so coolly, she begged the Master to upbraid her.

Now Mary had looked upon the occasion from another point of view. As soon as she saw Jesus come into the house she thought, 'What a privilege have I now to listen eagerly to such a teacher, and to treasure up his precious words! He is the Son of God, I will worship, I will adore, and every word he utters shall be stored in my memory.' She forgot the needs both of the Master and his followers, for her faith saw the inner glory which dwelt within him, and she was so overpowered with reverence, and so wrapt in devout wonder, that she became oblivious of all outward things. She had no faults to find with Martha for being so busy, she did not even think of Martha, she was altogether taken up with her Lord and with those gracious words which he was speaking. She had no will either, to censure or to praise or to think even of herself; everything was gone from her but her Lord and the word which he was uttering.

See ye then, that Martha was serving Christ, and so was Mary; Martha meant to honour Christ, so did Mary; they both agreed in their design, they differed in their way of carrying it out, and while Martha's service is not censured (only her being cumbered comes under the censure), yet Mary is expressly commended, as having chosen the good part; and therefore we do Martha no injustice if we show wherein she came short, and wherein Mary exceeded.

Our first observation will be this, the Martha spirit is very prevalent in the church of God just now; in the second place, the Martha spirit very much injures true service, in the third place, the Mary spirit is the source of the noblest form of consecration.

1. The Martha spirit is very prevalent in the church at this period – prevalent in some quarters to a mischievous degree, and among us all to a perilous extent. What do we intend by saying that the Martha spirit is prevalent just now? We mean first, that *there is a considerable tendency among Christian people, in serving Christ, to aim at making a fair show in the flesh.* Martha wanted to give our Lord right worthy entertainment which should be a credit to her house and to her family, and herein she is commendable far above those slovens who think anything good enough for Christ. So also, among professing Christians, there is at this present a desire to give to the cause of Christ buildings notable for their architecture and beauty. We must have no more barns, our meeting houses must exhibit our improving taste; if possible, our chapels must be correctly Gothic or sternly classical in all their details, both without and within. As to the service, we must cultivate the musical and the tasteful. We are exhorted not to be barely decent, but to aim at the sublime and beautiful. Our public worship, it is thought, should be impressive if not imposing; care should be taken that the music should be chaste, the singing conformed to the best rules of the art, and the preaching eloquent and attractive. So everything in connection with Christian labour should be made to appear generous and noble; by all means the subscription lists must be kept up; each denomination must excel the other in the amount of its annual funds; for surely everything done for Christ ought to be done in the best possible style.

Now in all this there is so much that is good, so much that is really intended to honour the Lord, that we see no room to censure: but yet show we unto you a more excellent way. These things ye may do, but there are higher things which ye must do, or suffer loss. Brethren, there is something better to be studied than the outward, for though this may be aimed at with a single eye to God's glory, and we judge no man, yet we fear the tendency is to imagine that mere externals are precious in the Master's sight. I trow he counts it a very small matter whether your house be a cathedral or a barn, to the Saviour it is small concern whether you have organs or whether you have not, whether you sing after the choicest rules of psalmody or no; he looks at your hearts, and if these ascend to him he accepts the praise. As for those thousands of pounds annually contributed, he estimates them not by the weights of the merchant but after the balances of the sanctuary. Your love expressed in your gifts he values, but what are the mere silver and gold to him? Funds, and encouraging accounts, and well-arranged machineries are well if they exist as the outgrowth of fervent love, but if they are the end-all, and the be-all, you miss the mark. Jesus would be better pleased with a grain of love than a heap of ostentatious service.

The Martha spirit shows itself *in the censuring of those persons who are careful about Christ's word*, who stand up for the doctrines of the gospel, who desire to maintain the ordinances as they were delivered unto them, and who are scrupulous and thoughtful, and careful concerning the truth as it is in Jesus. In newspapers, on platforms, and in common talk, you frequently hear earnest disciples of Jesus and consistent believers in his doctrines snubbed and denounced as unpractical. Theological questions are scouted as mere impertinences. Go in for ragged schools, certainly; reclaim the Arabs of the street, by all manner of means; pass a compulsory education bill, certainly; soup kitchens, free dinners, all excellent; we can all join in these; but never mention creeds and doctrines. Why, man, you cannot be aware of the enlightenment of our times! What importance can now be attached to mere biblical dogmas and ordinances? Why contend as to whether baptism shall be performed upon a babe or upon a believer, whether it shall be by sprinkling or by immersion? What matters the law of Christ in such a case? These things would do for the schoolmen of the dark ages to fight about, but what can be the importance of such trifles in this highly enlightened nineteenth century? Yes, that is the exaggeration of Martha. Mary, treasuring up every word of Christ, Mary counting each syllable a pearl, is reckoned to be unpractical, if not altogether idle. That spirit, I fear, is growing in these times, and needs to be checked; for, after all, there is truth and there is error, and charitable talk cannot alter the fact. To know and to love the gospel is no mean thing. Obedience to Jesus, and anxiety to learn his will so as to please him in all things, are not secondary matters.

Contemplation, worship, and growth in grace are not unimportant. I trust we shall not give way to the spirit which despises our Lord's teaching, for if we do, in prizing the fruit and despising the root we shall lose the fruit and the root too. In forgetting the great well-spring of holy activity, namely, personal piety, we shall miss the streams also. From the sincerity of faith and the fervour of love practical Christianity must arise; and if the food that faith and love feed upon be withdrawn, if sitting at the feet of Jesus be regarded as of secondary consequence, then both strength and will to serve the Lord will decline. I dread much the spirit which would tamper with truth for the sake of united action, or for any object under heaven – the latitudinarian spirit, which sneers at creeds and dogmas. Truth is no trifle. Not so thought our fathers, when at the stake they gave themselves to death, or on the brown heather of Scotland fell beneath the swords of Claverhouse's dragoons for truths which nowadays men count unimportant, but which, being truths, were to them so vital that they would sooner die than suffer them to be dishonoured. O for the same uncompromising love of truth! Would to God we could be both active and studious, and both learn with Mary and work with Martha!

The Martha spirit crops up *in our reckoning so many things necessary*. Martha believed that to make Christ an entertainment, there must be many things prepared; as to leaving one of those things out – it could not be. Our Lord would have been satisfied enough with the simplest fare – a piece of fish or of a honeycomb would well have contented him; but no, according to Martha's judgment there must be this, and there must be that. So is it with many good people now. They have their ideas of excellence, and if these cannot be realised they despair of doing anything acceptable for Christ.

I believe an educated ministry to be desirable, but none the less do I deplore the spirit which considers it to be essential. In the presence of the fishermen of Galilee we dare not subscribe to the necessity which with some is beyond doubt. You must not, according to the talk of some, allow these earnest young people to set about preaching, and your converted colliers and fiddlers should be stopped at once. The Holy Ghost has in all ages worked by men of his own choosing, but some churches would not let him if they could help it. Their pulpits are closed against the most holy and useful preachers, if they have not those many things with which the church nowadays cumbers her ministers and herself.

Then, my brethren, to carry on a good work, it is thought needful to have a society and large funds. I also approve of the society and the funds, I only regret that they should be so viewed as prime necessaries that few will stir without them. The idea of sending out a missionary with a few pounds in hand, as in the days of Carey, is set down in many quarters as absurd. How can you save souls without a committee? How can London be evangelised till you have raised at least a million of money? Can you hope to see men converted without an annual meeting in Exeter Hall? You must have a secretary – there is no moving an inch till he is elected; and know you not that without a committee ye can do nothing?

All these and a thousand things which time fails me to mention, are now deemed to be needful for the service of Jesus, until a true-hearted soul who could do much for his Lord, scarcely dares to move till he has put on Saul's armour of human patronage. O for apostolical simplicity, going everywhere preaching the word, and consecrating the labour of every believer to soul winning. To bring us back to first principles, 'one thing is needful,' and if by sitting at Jesus' feet we can find that one thing, it will stand us in better stead than all the thousand things which custom now demands. To catch the Spirit of Christ, to be filled with himself, this will equip us for godly labour as nothing else ever can. May all Christians yet come to put this one thing first and foremost, and count the power of deep piety to be the one essential qualification for holy work.

The censurable quality in the Martha spirit appears in *the satisfaction which many feel with more activity*. To have done so much preaching, or so much Sunday-school teaching, to have distributed so many tracts, to have made so many calls by our missionaries, all this seems to be looked at as end rather than means. If there be so much effort put forth, so much work done, is it not enough? Our reply is, it is not enough, it is nothing without the divine blessing. Brethren, where mere work is prized, and the inner life forgotten, prayer comes to be at a discount. The committee is attended, but the devotion meeting forsaken. The gathering together for supplication is counted little compared with the collecting of subscriptions. The opening prayer at public meetings is regarded as a very proper thing, but there are those who regard it as a mere formality, which might be very well laid aside, and, therefore, invariably come in after prayer is over. It will be an evil day for us when we trust in the willing and the running, and practically attempt to do without the Holy Spirit.

This lofty estimate of mere activity, for its own sake, throws the acceptance of our work into the shade. The Martha spirit says, if the work is done, is not that all? The Mary spirit asks whether Jesus is well pleased or no? All must be done in his name and by his Spirit, or nothing is done. Restless service, which sits not at his feet, is but the clattering of a mill which turns without grinding corn; it is but an elaborate method of doing nothing. I do not want less activity – how earnestly do I press you to it almost every Sabbath day; but I do pray that we may feel that all our strength lies in God, and that we can only be strong as we are accepted of Christ, and only can be accepted in Christ as we wait upon him in prayer, trust him, and live upon him. Ye may compass sea and land to make your proselytes, but if ye have not the Spirit of Christ ye are none of his. Ye may rise up early and sit up late, and eat the bread of sorrows, but unless ye trust in the Lord your God ye shall not prosper. The joy of the Lord is your strength. They that wait on the Lord shall renew their strength. Without Christ ye can do nothing. Hath he not told you, 'He that abideth in me, and I in him, the same bringeth forth much fruit'? Was it not written of old, 'I am like a green fir tree: from me is thy fruit found'?

Once more, Martha's spirit is predominant in the church of God to a considerable extent now, *in the evident respect which is paid to the manifest, and the small regard which is given to the secret.* All regenerated persons ought to be workers for God and with God, but let the working never swamp the believing, never let the servant be more prominent than the son; never, because you conduct a class, or are chief man at a village station, forget that you are a sinner saved by grace, and have need still to be looking to the Crucified, and finding all your life in him. You lose your strength as a worker if you forget your dependence as a believer. To labour for Christ is a pleasant thing, but beware of doing it mechanically; and this you can only prevent by diligently cultivating personal communion with Christ.

My brother, it may be you will undertake so much service that your time will be occupied, and you will have no space for prayer and reading the Word. The half-hour in the morning for prayer will be cut short, and the time allotted for communion with God in the evening will be gradually intrenched upon by this engagement and the other occupation, and when this is the case I tremble for you. You are killing the steed by spurring it and denying it food; you are undermining your house by drawing out the stones from the foundation to pile them at the top. You are doing your soul serious mischief if you put the whole of your strength into that part of your life which is visible to men, and forget that portion of your life which is secret between you and your God.

To gather up all in one, I fear there is a great deal among us of religious activity of a very inferior sort; it concerns itself with, the external of service, it worries itself with merely human efforts, and it attempts in its own strength to achieve divine results. The real working which God will accept is that which goes hand in hand with a patient waiting upon Christ, with heart searching, with supplication, with communion, with a childlike dependence upon Jesus, with a firm adhesion to his truth, with an intense love to his person, and an abiding in him at all seasons; may we have more of such things. Martha's spirit, though excellent in itself so far as it goes, must not overshadow Mary's quiet, deep-seated piety, or evil will come of it.

2. Secondly, we observe that *The Martha Spirit Injures True Service*.

Service may be true, and yet somewhat marred upon the wheel. Give your attention not so much to what I say, as to the bearing of it upon yourselves. It may be that you will find, as we speak, that you have been verily guilty touching these things. The Martha spirit *brings the least welcome offering to Christ*. It is welcome, but it is the least welcome. Our Lord Jesus when on earth was more satisfied by conversing to a poor Samaritan woman than he would have been by the best meat and drink. In carrying on his spiritual work he had meat to eat, that his disciples knew not of. Evermore his spiritual nature was predominant over his physical nature, and those persons who brought him spiritual gifts brought him the gifts which he preferred. Here then was Martha's dish of well-cooked meat, but there was Mary's gift of a humble obedient heart; here was Martha decking the table, but there was Mary submitting her judgment to the Lord, and looking up with wondering eyes as she heard his matchless speech. Mary was bringing to Jesus the better offering. With Martha, he would in his condescension be pleased, but in Mary be found satisfaction. Martha's service he accepted benevolently, but Mary's worship he accepted with complacency. Now, brethren and sisters, all that you can give to Christ in any shape or form will not be so dear to him as the offering of your fervent love, the clinging of your humble faith, the reverence of your adoring souls. Do not, I pray you, neglect the spiritual for the sake of the external, or else you will be throwing away gold to gather to yourself iron, you will be pulling down the palaces of marble that you may build for yourselves hovels of clay.

Martha's spirit has this mischief about it also, that *it brings self too much to remembrance.* We would not severely judge Martha, but we conceive that in some measure she aimed at making the service a credit to herself as the mistress of the house; at any rate, self came up when she began to grow weary, and complained that she was left to serve alone. We also want our work to show well as our work; we like those who see it to commend it, and if none commend it we feel that we are hardly done by, and are left to work alone. Now, to the extent in which I think of myself in my service I spoil it. Self must sink, and Christ be all in all. John the Baptist's saying must be our motto, 'He must increase, I must decrease;' for Jesus' shoe latchet we are not worthy to unloose. Too much work and too little fellowship will always bring self into prominence. Self must be prayed down, and fellowship with Jesus must keep it down.

Martha seemed to fancy *that what she was doing was needful for Christ.* She was cumbered about much serving, because she thought it necessary that there should be a noble entertainment for the Lord. We are all too apt to think that Jesus wants our work, and that he cannot do without us. The preacher enquires what would become of the church if he were removed! The deacon is suspicious that if he were taken away there would be a great gap left in the executive of the church; the teacher of a class feels that those children would never be converted, Christ would miss of the travail of his soul but for him. Ah, but a fly on St Paul's Cathedral might as well imagine that all the traffic at his feet was regulated by his presence, and would cease should he remove. I love you to think that Christ will do much work by you, and to attach as much weight as you can to your responsibilities, but as to Jesus needing us – the thing is preposterous.

Mary is much wiser when she feels, 'He desires me to receive his words, and yield him my love; I would gladly give him meat, but he will see to that; he is the Master of all things, and can do without me or Martha. I need him far more than he can need me.' We spoil our service when we over-estimate its importance, for this leads us into loftiness and pride. Martha, under the influence of this high temper, came to complain of her sister, and to complain of her Lord too, as if he were excusing her idleness. 'Dost thou not care that my sister hath left me to serve alone?' How it spoils what we do for Christ when we go about it with a haughty spirit; when we feel 'I can do this, and it is grand to do that; am not I somewhat better than others? Must not my Master think well of me?' The humble worker wins the day. God accepts the man who feels his nothingness, and out of the depths cries to him; but the great ones he will put down from their seat, and send the rich ones empty away. Activity, if not balanced by devotion, tends to puff us up, and so to prevent acceptance with God.

Martha also fell into *an unbelieving vexation*. Her idea of what was necessary to be done was so great that she found she could not attain to it. There must be this side dish, and there must be that principal joint, there must be this meat and that wine, it must be cooked just so many minutes, this must be done to a turn, and so on, and so on, and so on, and so on; and now time flies, she fears yonder guest has been slighted; that servant is not back from the market; many things go wrong when you are most anxious to have them right. You good housewives, who may have had large parties to prepare for, know what these cares mean, I dare say; and something of the sort troubled Martha, so that she became fretful and unbelieving. She had a work to do beyond her strength as she thought, and her faith failed her, and her unbelief went petulantly to complain to her Lord.

Have we never erred in the same way? We must have that Sunday school excellently conducted, that morning prayer-meeting must be improved, that Bible class must be revived, our morning sermon must be a telling one, and so on! The preacher here speaks of himself, for he sometimes feels that there is too much responsibility laid upon his shoulders, and he is very apt in reviewing his great field of labour to grow desponding in spirit. But when the preacher confessed that he spoke of himself, he only did so because he represents his fellow workers, and you also grow faint and doubtful. Alas! in such a case, the enjoyment of service evaporates, the fretfulness which pines over details spoils the whole, and the worker becomes a mere drudge and scullion instead of an angel who does God's commandments, hearkening unto the voice of his word. Instead of glowing and burning like seraphs, our chariot wheels are taken off by our anxiety, and we drag heavily. Faith it is that secures acceptance, but when unbelief comes in, the work falls flat to the ground.

At such times when the man or the church shall become subject to the Martha spirit, *the voluntary principle falls a little into disrepute.* I believe the voluntary principle is the worst thing in all the world to work where there is no grace, but where there is grace it is the one principle that God accepts. Now, Martha would have Mary made to serve Christ. What right has she to be sitting down there? Whether she likes or not she must get up and wait like her sister. Martha's voluntary desire to do much, leads her to think that Mary, if she has not quite such a voluntary love for the work, must be driven to it, must have a sharp word from Christ about it. So it is with us. We are so willing to contribute to the Lord's work, that we wish we had ten thousand times as much to give. Our heart is warm within us, and we feel we would make no reserve, and then are grieved with others because they give so very little, and we wish we could compel them to give. And so we would put their cankered money into the same treasury with the bright freewill offerings of the saints, as if the Lord would receive such beggarly pittances squeezed out by force in the same manner as he accepts the voluntary gifts of his people. It were wiser if we left those unwilling contributions to rust in the pockets of their owners, for in the long run I believe they do not help the cause, for only that which is given out of a generous spirit, and out of love to Christ, will come up accepted before him. Too readily do we get away from the free spirit when we get away from the right spirit. The fact is, the Martha spirit spoils all, because it gets us away from the inner soul of service, as I have said before, to the mere husks of service; we cease to do work as to the Lord, we labour too much for the service's sake; the main thing in our minds is the service, and not the Master; we are cumbered, and he is forgotten.

Thus have I indicated as briefly as I could some of the weaknesses of the Martha spirit.

3. Now for *The Mary Spirit*. I have to show you that it is capable of producing the noblest form of consecration to Christ. Its noblest results will not come just yet. Martha's fruits ripen very quickly, Mary's take time. When Lazarus was dead, you will remember Martha ran to meet Christ, but Mary sat still in the house; Martha wanted her own time, Mary could take Christ's time. So after awhile, just before our Lord's death, we find that Mary did a grand action, she did what Martha never thought of doing, she brought forth a box of precious ointment and poured it on the Lord's head, and anointed him with ointment. While she was sitting at Christ's feet, she was forming and filling the springs of action. You are not losing time while you are feeding the soul. While by contemplation you are getting purpose strengthened and motive purified, you are rightly using time. When the man becomes intense, when he gets within him principles vital, fervent, energetic, then when the season for work comes he will work with a power and a result which empty people can never attain however busy they may be. If the stream flows at once, as soon as ever there is a shower, it must be little better than a trickling rivulet; but if the current stream is dammed up, so that for awhile nothing pours down the river bed, you will in due time, when the waters have gathered strength, witness a torrent before which nothing can stand. Mary was filling up the fountain head, she was listening and learning, feeding, edifying, loving, and growing strong. The engine of her soul was getting its steam ready, and when all was right her action was prompt and forcible. *Meanwhile, the manner of her action was being refined.*

Martha's actions were good, but, if I may use the word, they were commonplace, she must make a great feed for the Lord Jesus, just as for any earthly friend; the spiritual nature of Christ she had forgotten, she was providing nothing for it; but Mary's estimate of Christ was of a truer order; she looked at him as a priest, she viewed him as a prophet, she adored him as a king, and she had heard him speak about dying, and had listened to his testimony about suffering, and dimly guessing what it meant, she prepared the precious spikenard that ere the dying should come she might anoint him. The woman's deed was full of meaning and of instruction; it was indeed an embodied poem; the odour that filled the house was the perfume of love and elevated thought. She became refined in her actions by the process of musing and learning. Those who think not, who meditate not, who commune not with Christ, will do commonplace things very well, but they will never rise to the majesty of a spiritual conception, or carry out a heart-suggested work for Christ.

That sitting of Mary was also creating *originality of art*. I tried two Sabbaths ago to enforce upon you the duty of originality of service as the right thing, that as we wandered everyone in his own way we should each serve God in his own way, according to our peculiar adaptation and circumstances. Now this blessed woman did so. Martha is in a hurry to be doing something – she does what any other admirer of Jesus would do, she prepares meat and a festival; but Mary does what but one or two besides herself would think of – she anoints him, and is honoured in the deed. She struck out a spark of light from herself as her own thought, and she cherished that spark till it became a flaming act. I would that in the church of God we had many sisters at Jesus' feet who at last would start up under an inspiration and say, 'I have thought of something, that will bring glory to God which the church has not heard of before, and this will I put in practice, that there may be a fresh gem in my Redeemer's crown.'

This sitting at the Master's feet guaranteed *the real spirituality of what she did.* Did you notice when I read what the Master said concerning the pouring of the ointment upon him, '*She hath kept* this for my burial'? He praised her for keeping it, as well as for giving it. I suppose that for months she had set apart that particular ointment, and held it in reserve. Much of the sweetest aroma of a holy work lies in its being thought over and brought out with deliberation. There are works to be done at once and straightaway, but there are some other works to be weighed and considered. What shall I do my Saviour to praise? There is a cherished scheme, there is a plan, the details of which shall be prayed out, and every single part of it sculptured in the imagination and realised in the heart, and then the soul shall wait, delighting herself in prospect of the deed, until the dear purpose may be translated into fact. It is well to wait, expectantly saying, 'Yes, the set time will come, I shall be able to do the deed, I shall not go down to my grave altogether without having been serviceable; it is not yet the time, it is not yet the appropriate season, and I am not quite ready for it myself, but I will add grace to grace and virtue to virtue, and I will add self-denial to self-denial, till I am fit to accomplish the one chosen work.' So the Saviour praised Mary that she had kept this; kept it till the fit moment came before his burial; and then, but not till then, she had poured out and revealed her love.

Ay, it is not your thoughtless service, performed while your souls are half asleep; it is that which you do for Christ with eyes that overflow, with hearts that swell with emotion, it is this that Jesus accepts. May we have more of such service, as we shall have if we have more of sitting at his feet. Christ accepted her, he said she had chosen the good part which should not be taken from her; and if our work be spiritual, intense, fervent, thoughtful, if it spring out of fellowship, if it be the outgushing of deep principles, of inward beliefs, of solemn gratitudes, then our piety shall never be taken from us, it will be an enduring thing, and not like the mere activities of Martha, things that come and go.

I have thus wrought out my text. I shall utter but two or three words upon the general applications of it. I shall apply it to three or four things very briefly. Brethren, I believe in our Nonconformity; I believe if ever England wanted Nonconformists it is now; but there is a tendency to make Nonconformity become a thing of externals, dealing with state and church and politics. The political relations of Nonconformists, I believe in their value, I would not have a man less earnest upon them, but I am always fearful lest we should forget that Nonconformity is nothing if it be not spiritual, and that the moment we, as Dissenters, become merely political or formal, it is all over with us. Our strength is at the Master's feet, and I am afraid for our Nonconformity if it lives elsewhere. I mark so much conformity to the world, so much laxity of rule, so much love of novel opinions, that I tremble. I would we could go back to Puritanism. We are getting too lax, there is too much worldliness and carnality among us. There is little fear of our being censured, even by the world, for being too particular. I am afraid we are too much like the world for the world to hate us. As I pray that Nonconformity may always prevail in England, so I earnestly pray that she may stand because she abides near to Christ, holds his truth, prizes his word, and lives upon himself.

Now the like is true of *missions*. Apply the principle there. God bless missions; our prayer goes up for them as warmly as for our soul's salvation. When shall the utmost ends of the earth behold the salvation of our God! But the strength of missions must lie not so much in arrangements, in committees, in moneys, in men, as in waiting upon the Christ of God. We shall not do any more with a hundred thousand pounds than with a single thousand, unless we get more grace; we shall not have more souls won with fifty missionaries than with five, unless we get ten times the amount of power from the right hand of the Most High. The waking up in missions needs to begin in our prayer meetings, and in our churches; in our personal wrestlings with God for the conversion of the heathen must lie the main strength of the workers that go out to do the deed. Let us remember this, Mary shall yet pour the box of ointment upon the head of the Anointed, Martha cannot do it.

The same thing is true in revivals. Persons will talk about getting up a revival – of all things I do believe one of the most detestable of transactions. 'If you want a revival of religion,' it is said, 'you must get Mr So-and-so to preach' – with him I suppose is the residue of the Spirit. Oh, but if you want a revival, you must adopt the methods so long in vogue, and so well known as connected with such-and-such a revival! I suppose the Spirit of God is no more a free Spirit, then, as he used to be in the olden times; and whereas of old he breathed where he listed, you fancy your methods and plans can control him. It is not so; it is not so in any degree. The way to get the revival is to begin at the Master's feet; you must go there with Mary and afterwards you may work with Martha. When every Christian's heart is acting right by feeding on Christ's word and drinking in Christ's Spirit, then will the revival come. When we had the long drought, some farmers watered their grass, but found it did but very little good. An Irish gentleman remarked in my hearing that he had always noticed that when it rained there were clouds about, and so all the air was in right order for the descent of rain. We have noticed the same, and it so happens that the clouds and general constitution of the atmosphere have much to do with the value of moisture for the herbs. It is no good watering them in the sun, the circumstances do not benefit them. So with revivals. Certain things done under certain circumstances become abundantly useful, but if you have not similar circumstances, you may use the same machinery, but mischief instead of good will follow. Begin yourself with the Master, and then go outward to his service, but plans of action must be secondary.

So too, lastly, if you *want to serve God*, as I trust you do, I charge you first be careful of your own souls; do not begin with learning how to preach, or how to teach, or how to do this and that; dear friend, get the strength within your own soul, and then even if you do not know how to use it scientifically, yet you will do much. The first thing is, get the heart warmed, stir up your manhood, brace up all your faculties, get the Christ within you, ask the everlasting God to come upon you, get him to inspire you, and then if your methods should not be according to the methods of others it will not matter, or if they should, neither will it be of consequence, having the power you will accomplish the results. But if you go about to perform the work before you have the strength from on high, you shall utterly fail. Better things we hope of you. God send them. Amen.

4

Concentration and Diffusion[1]

Then took Mary a pound of ointment of spikenard,
very costly, and anointed the feet of Jesus, and wiped
his feet with her hair: and the house was filled with
the odour of the ointment.

John 12:3

You will notice, if you read the narrative attentively, that the two sisters and the brother, who made up the favoured household at Bethany, though all most truly loving Jesus, had each one a different way of showing that love. Even so, true children of God do not always feel moved to serve the Lord Jesus in the same fashion, or to express their love to him in precisely the same manner.

---

1. This sermon was preached at the Metropolitan Tabernacle, Newington and was published 9 December 1909.

Martha served: she was the housekeeper, and with much diligence made him a supper. It would have been a sad omission had there been no table spread for so blessed a guest, and who could prepare it so well as Martha? Sometimes we have heard people speak disparagingly of Martha, but, truly they mistake the Lord, who never chided her for serving but for being on one occasion so cumbered by it as to think hardly of her sister. Martha, in this instance, did not fall into the fault which her Lord once so gently chided; she did her part quietly and well, and thereby set forth her attachment to Jesus in the most commendable manner.

We have sisters in the church whose way of serving Christ is in the household, or by caring for the sick and the poor; like Dorcas, they make garments for them, or like holy women of old, they minister to the Lord of their substance. Their work is with things temporal, but they are none the less approved of their loving Master. Brethren, too, as deacons, may better honour the Lord by serving tables than they could by attempting to edify saints when the gifts suitable for that work are denied them. Each man and woman must labour according to his or her ability and calling.

As for Lazarus, he was 'one of them that sat at the table'. We might hastily imagine that by sitting there he did nothing: but, my brethren, the people had come together very much to see Lazarus, who had been raised from the dead; and for him to sit there, and to show himself, and especially to eat and to drink, was to do the best thing to convince onlookers that he was indeed alive. Our blessed Lord himself, when he rose from the dead, found it needful to convince his disciples that he was really alive and in a real body, and therefore he took a piece of a broiled fish and of a honeycomb, and did eat before them all. When they saw him eat, then they were sure that he lived. So, when Lazarus ate at the table, sceptics could not say, 'It is merely his corpse, set upright to look like life, or a mere phantom to deceive.' Lazarus eating and drinking was a testimony for Jesus, and I would that we all knew how even to eat and drink to the glory of God. There are some Christians who cannot do much or say much, but their godly lives, their patient suffering, their quiet holiness, are good witnesses to Jesus. I have looked at the lilies and the roses in the garden, and I have thought, 'You toil not, neither do you spin, you preach not, neither do you sing, and yet you praise my Lord, simply *by being beautiful*, and by unconsciously shedding abroad the perfume which he gives you.'

May not some saints be glorifying God most truly though they can do no more than this? Besides, some one of the family was needed to keep the Master company, and preside as host at the table, and who could do this but Lazarus, the master of the house? Anywhere else, Lazarus might have been out of place, but to me it appears most seemly that Lazarus should sit at the table; and if he modestly declined to take the head of it, and sat with others, still he was bound to be there.

But what shall Mary do? She need not be at the table, Lazarus was there; she is, perhaps, of small use in the kitchen, her abilities are slender in that direction. What shall Mary do? Her heart was very warm, and she felt she must do something. She did not ask anybody, however, for her own mind was inventive. She knew that it was a usual custom with honoured guests to anoint them with ointment; she perceived that this had not yet been done, or if done, not in the royal style which her love suggested. Perhaps she was very lovely, and had been somewhat fond of adorning her person; her long hair may have been much cherished, and she may have been profuse in the use of perfume upon it; the thought strikes her, she will consecrate that hair to Jesus, and that pound of fragrant unguent which she had stored up for the beautifying of herself shall be spent upon *him*. It was very costly, but it had not cost a penny too much now that it could be used upon *him*. There was a pound of it, but there was none too much for *him*. It was very sweet, but none too sweet for *him*. She brings the pound of ointment, and pours it upon his feet as he lies reclining at the table, and then begins to wipe his feet with the hairs of her head, consecrating her personal beauty as well as her valued treasure to him whom she both loved and adored. She had found something to do, and that something not the least of the three works of love.

The service of the three members of that elect family made up a complete feast; Martha prepared the supper, Lazarus conversed with their honoured guest, and Mary anointed the Master's feet. Judge you not, one another, my brothers and sisters; do each one what you feel you can do, and what the Lord expects of you, and look not on another's work with ungenerous eyes. Neither Martha, nor Lazarus, nor Mary, complained of each other, but together they made the service complete. All members have not the same office, but each one must lovingly supplement the office of the rest, and emulation and jealousy must never enter among us.

We will now forget the others, and look alone at Mary. We are struck with the service which she performed for Christ. It was somewhat singular, it was very demonstrative, and it proved her love to be of no common kind. Other women besides Martha had made him a supper; other hosts besides Lazarus had sat at the table with him; but no other had anointed his feet exactly in her fashion, though perhaps some may have come near to it.

Mary was inventive, demonstrative, patient, ardent, enthusiastic. What she did was the deed of a soul all on fire, the deed of a woman filled with deep devotion and reverent love. There is an old proverb that 'still waters run deep'. Mary had these still waters within her heart; she sat at Jesus' feet, and heard his words; she was a woman of few words, but of many thoughts; she considered, she pondered, and she adored. Mary among women is the counterpart of John among men and perhaps, at this time, she had even outrun the beloved disciple in quick discernment of the Lord's true nature. It seems to me that she had perceived his Godhead, and understood more of what he was and what he was about to do than any other of the disciples did; at least I can on that theory better understand her deed of love. She devised a homage for him which she would not have dreamed of presenting to any other than such a one as she perceived the Lord to be. Pondering many things within her soul, and withal remembering what he had done for her personally, and for her dear brother Lazarus, whom she loved so well she determined that a special mark of reverential homage should be paid him, and she carried out the resolve. Deep thought led to burning love, and burning love led to immediate action.

Beloved friends, the Church of Christ needs a band of men and women full of enthusiasm who will go beyond others in devotion to the Lord Jesus. We need missionaries who will dare to die to carry the gospel to regions beyond;

we need ministers who will defy public opinion, and with flaming zeal burn a way into men's hearts; we need men and women who will consecrate all that they have by daring deeds of heroic self-sacrifice. Oh, that all Christians were like this, but we must at least have some. We need a bodyguard of loving champions to rally around the Saviour, the bravest of the brave, Immortals and Invincibles, who shall lead the van of the armies of the Lord. Where are we to get them? How are they to be produced?

The Holy Spirit's way to train men and women who shall greatly serve Christ is to lead them to deep thought and quiet contemplation; thence they obtain the knowledge and vital principle, which are the fuel of true zeal. You cannot leap into high devotion, neither can you be preached into it, nor dream yourself into it, or be electrified into it by revivalism. It must, through the divine energy of the Holy Spirit, arise out of hard, stern dealing with your soul, and near and dear communion with your Saviour. You must sit at his feet, or you will never anoint them; he must pour his divine teaching into you, or you will never pour out a precious ointment upon him.

This is a rather long introduction, but we will now leave it all, and crave your attention for a little time to a short parable which appears to me to grow out of this incident. Mary took a pound of ointment, and poured it all on Christ's feet; that is *concentration*. When she had poured it all out on Christ's feet, the whole house was filled with the odour of the ointment; that is *diffusion*, and the surest way to effective diffusion is perfect concentration.

1. Let us speak a little first upon this *Concentration*. You want, my friend, to do something before you die, which may

prove a blessing to your family connections. The desire is good, but do not begin with diffusion; commence with concentration, and let Mary be your model. She brought out all her ointment, the whole pound without reserve. Even so, consecrate to the Saviour all that you have: every faculty, power, possession and ability. Half the pound of spikenard would not have sufficed. That half-pound in reserve would have spoiled the deed. Perhaps we should never have heard of it at all if it had been less complete. Half a heart given to Christ? Tell it not in Gath, whisper it not in the streets of Askelon. Half a life given to Christ? Half your faculties, half your powers given to Christ? It is an unworthy gift; he gave you all, and he claims all of you. O dear soul, if thou wouldst fill the house with sweet odour, bring in thy whole self, and pour out thy heart at his feet!

Note that, as she brought all, so *she poured it all upon Jesus*. She had no fear of the black looks of Judas, for the act was not meant for Judas; it was all for Jesus. I do not think she gave a thought to Martha, or Lazarus, or to any of them. The whole pound was for Jesus. The highest way of living is to live for Jesus, and altogether for Jesus, not caring what this man saith or how the other judgeth, but feeling that as *he* hath bought us with his blood, and we are his from the crown of our head to the sole of our foot, we therefore own no master but our Redeemer.

Brothers and sisters, do you live for Jesus in that fashion? Do we not perform many actions under the impulse of secondary motives? I like, for my part, sometimes to do an act of which I feel, 'I do not consider whether this will benefit my fellow men. I am doing it alone for Jesus. What comes of it, whether a soul shall be saved or not, is not my main care; but I am speaking this good word in his honour, and if God accepts it, and it glorifies Jesus, my end is served.' Oh, it is a blessed thing to feel that you are living, not as a servant of man, nor of the church, nor of a sect, or party, but of him whose precious blood has bought you!

Concentrate all your faculties upon the Lord himself, and then consult not with flesh and blood. Mary did not wait for any advice about the matter. There is Jesus, and there are his blessed feet, inviting her to anoint them. She will not stop to enquire what Martha thinks, much less what Judas murmurs, but her heart tells her to do it. All her powers of love say to her, 'Do it,' and she brings out the costly perfume, and pours it all on him.

When the criticism is given about the wasteful deed, she cares not to make an apology, and she needs not to do so. If for the moment the grumbling grated harshly upon her ear, her Master's look of love and that kind word, 'Let her alone; against the day of my burying hath she kept this,' are quite enough for her. She did not aim at pleasing Judas; and so, if Judas is not pleased, she is not disappointed; she did it for Jesus, and Jesus being pleased, she has gained all that she sought for. Ah, brethren, this is what we must try to do; we must not always remain in leading-strings, asking other people what they think about our actions; if we know that a certain course is right, let us follow it, and let others think and say what they choose.

This concentration of everything upon Jesus is the only way of worthily serving him. When we give him all, we do not give him a thousandth part of what he deserves; but to give him half – to give him a tithe, to give him what we can easily spare – is a poor way of expressing our love to him. Who else deserves a part of your service? If you have been redeemed from death and hell, who else can claim a portion of your heart? Look at him in his life of labour, look at him on the cross, and look at him remembering you still before the throne of God. Does he not engross your affections? Say, does he not throw another cord of love around you, and bind you as a sacrifice to the horns of the altar? I will not linger longer on that point. Enough is as good as a feast. Concentrate, concentrate, concentrate, concentrate all on Jesus.

2. Now, consider what will come of it; namely, *Diffusion*. 'The house was filled with the odour of the ointment.' Mark that the house was not filled with the odour of the ointment through Mary's seeking. She did not run into every chamber, and drop a little on the floor, so that every room might smell of it; she did not care whether the house was perfumed or not, she only wanted to anoint her Lord, and therefore she poured all the ointment on his feet. The result was that, the rooms were perfumed, but that was not her main object. She did not tell everybody that she had precious ointment in store, but they know it by her pouring it out. Whenever you hear a man boast that he is holy, remember that good scent needs no proclaiming. The only cart I ever meet with that rings a bell is the dust cart. If jewels and diamonds, or the bullion of the Bank of England, are carried through the streets, no bell is rung. 'Great cry and little wool' is a proverb which has had a new exposition in this country of late; a wonderful cry about holiness and wonderful little holiness to cry about, but a great deal to be wept over and lamented before the living God.

To stand in every room, and cry, 'Spikenard! Spikenard! Wonderful spikenard!' would have been idle. Pour it on

Jesus' feet, and you will not have to say anything about it, for every room will be sweet with the smell thereof. We need, nowadays, dear friends, to have a little less talk about what men are and much more actual living unto Jesus. The Lord works it in us by his Spirit!

Why was it that Mary's spikenard did perfume all the house, and how is it that, if there is true grace in a man's life, it is sure to be felt and recognized without his saying much about it? We reply, *because it is real*. Real religion is always influential: sham religion has but sham power. You cannot get influence by saying, 'I mean to influence So-and-so;' as well hope to stop the sun and moon without Joshua's miraculous power. The power of religion within yourself will be very much the measure of the power which you exercise over others. Artificial flowers may be made so exactly like the real plants that you can scarcely detect them, but they lack the perfume of our garden favourites; and so also the mere professor has not the fragrance of real grace, and consequently no attractive and sweetening influence upon others; but where religion is real, true, heartfelt, deep – where there is strong, all-absorbing love to Christ – the sweet perfume of grace will give the man influence over his fellow men. I cannot tell you how it is that a man who lives near to God has this influence, but I know he has it. The camphor tree is full of camphor in all parts of it, branch, bark, root, and flower are all full of camphor; and the man who really lives for Jesus is full of gracious influence in all places and times. May you and I be so!

How was it that the rooms became filled with the odour? There is a law of nature which chemists call *the law of transfusion*. If two gases of an entirely different nature are brought into contact, they commence at once to mix with one another, and continue to unite till they are thoroughly intermingled. Thus flavours and odours diffuse themselves in the air. It is so with good and evil in the world. Insensibly, every man is the worse for coming in contact with a vicious example; and consciously or unconsciously, every man is swayed to some degree for good by the presence of a virtuous life. The law of transfusion enters into moral and spiritual matters, as well as into the realm of chemistry; and if you walk with God, and endeavour to preserve a blameless life, and glorify Christ, influence will be yours without your seeking it. How far it will extend, God alone knows. It may reach far beyond what you suppose to be its sphere, and may even teach some who are yet unborn, who shall hear from others how you lived, and how you glorified Christ.

Besides, dear friends, true piety is a very powerful essence, and *possesses great energy*. There are perfumes in nature, like the attar of roses, of which the smallest drop will make a chamber smell for many a day: true holiness is such a mighty, pervading essence that if you possess it, it cannot be hidden, it will make itself known as a sweet savour even as far as heaven. The life of God is in it, and it must operate. In everything that is good, God lieth hidden. The Spirit of God dwells in every gracious word, and godly thought, and holy deed, and he is sweetness itself. The name of Jesus is as ointment poured forth, what must his Spirit be? Yet that Spirit is to be found in every true believer.

I want to close by asking you, dear friends, how far, as yet, you have concentrated your love upon Christ, and thus have influenced those who dwell in your house: I will only ask about your own house. Has your house been filled with the odour of the ointment? You do pray, but have your prayers been so mighty with God that they have brought, down a blessing upon your family? You seek to avoid sin, you try to make your conversation pure, gracious, kind, cheerful, loving, and Christlike; do you think that some in your house have been blessed thereby? I do not ask, 'Have all been converted?' for, though all the house was the better for Mary's ointment, yet Judas remained a traitor. I should not wonder if some in your house may have even disliked you the more, for your piety; but, still, the Lord frequently blesses godliness, and makes it the means of conversion.

O woman, thou mayest gain thy husband by thy piety; if he will not hear sermons, he will hear that quiet, loving life of thine! O sister, thou mayest win thy brother by thy love; he will not read pious books, but those letters of thine, those sweet words of tender rebuke and invitation, he does read them, and he feels them too, though you fear he does not! Father, those boys of yours are not yet what you could wish, but they must feel your godly example. Perhaps, when you lie beneath the sod, they will recollect what you used to be. Fill the house with the odour of true religion. Fill the parlour and the drawing-room, the bed-chamber and the kitchen, with hallowed conversation. I say again, not with mere talk and Pharisaic pretence, but with real holy living and true godly communion; and, depend upon it, you are doing for your children and your servants the best thing in your power to do. Give them teaching, give them warning and entreaty; but, still, the actual perfuming with godliness must arise from your own holy living, it must be begotten of the ointment poured on Jesus' feet.

Ah, dear friends, I wish that, not only the house in which we may happen to dwell, but the workshop where we labour, the shop where we trade, the place of business where we associate with others, might all be perfumed with grace. Christian men are not to glide out of the way of their fellow creatures and shut themselves up in order to be pious any more than a soldier may hope to win the battle by running away. No, mix with your fellow men. If there are offices of trust to discharge, do not leave them to the lowest of the low to discharge them, but be willing to do public service for your country; but so do this that you shall spread abroad in every office the savour of honesty and integrity, and make the rogue and the cheat ashamed of themselves. I would to God that every Christian church were a living protest against all the wrongdoing of the times, a gracious disinfectant, to stay the abounding corruption. There is an evil smell of sin perpetually reeking towards heaven, and it needs that you Christian men should live Christlike lives in public as well as in private until you fill this country with a healthier savour, and until England shall become a Christian country in fact as well as in name. Would God that the example of Christians might yet become so potent that all nations might feel its power, that wars might cease, that cruelties of every kind might come to an end, and that the sweet savour of Jesus' name, manifested through his people, might perfume the whole world as though God had showered upon it ambrosia, essences and fragrances from the flowers of heaven to sweeten it against the time when Christ himself shall come, and make it a marriage chamber for his chosen bride! God grant that the perfume of your holiness may reach the stars; that your lives may be so sweet that, beyond these fogs and clouds, the sweet aroma of your grace may rise acceptable to God through Jesus Christ, for we are ever a sweet savour unto him if we live unto the Lord.

I fear me, however, that I may be addressing some whose lives are not a sweet perfume at all. Ah, take heed to yourselves! If you are living without God and without Christ, if you are living in any secret sin, take heed to yourselves. You may think that you will be able to conceal the ill savour of your sin, but you will not. How wonderfully does evil tell its own secret! The intolerable effluvium of many a secret sin has forced its way to notice. Beware thou who wouldst cover thy sin! Beware, I pray thee. For the task is hopeless. Dig, dig, dig, dig deep, and in the dead of night cover up the sin, but like the blood of Abel, it crieth from the ground. 'Be sure your sin will find you out.'

If you are living now in sin, and yet pretend to be virtuous, remember that, if your hypocrisy is never found out in this life, it will confront you at the last great day. How terrible will be the resurrection of buried sins to men who know not Christ! They will wake up in the next world, and find their sins howling around them like grim wolves, insatiable, fierce, and terrible. Any one sin is able to destroy the soul, but what must it be to be surrounded by thousands, howling with terrible voices, and eager to drag you down, and tear you in pieces? It will be so with you, sirs, it must be so with many of you, unless you lay hold now upon the great salvation. Jesus Christ can drive away those wolves, can stay the ill savour of your sins. If you will trust him, if you will yield your hearts to him, he will deliver you; but if you will not, on your own heads be your blood.

5

Over Against the Sepulchre[1]

Sitting over against the sepulchre.
Matthew 27:61

Mary Magdalene and the other Mary were last at the Saviour's grave. They had associated themselves with Joseph and Nicodemus in the sad but loving task of placing the body of their Lord in the silent tomb, and after the holy men had gone home they lingered still near the grave. Sitting down, perhaps upon some seat in the garden, or on some projection of

---

1. Preached on Sunday morning, March 24th, 1878, at the Metropolitan Tabernacle, Newington.

the rock, they waited in mournful solitude. They had seen where and how the body was laid, and so had done their utmost, but yet they sat watching still; love has never done enough, it is hungry to render service. They could scarcely take their eyes away from the spot which held their most precious treasure, nor leave till they were compelled to do so the sacred relics of their Best Beloved.

The Virgin Mary had been taken by John to his own home. She had sustained too great a shock to remain at the tomb, for in her were fulfilled the words, 'Yea, a sword shall pierce through thine own heart also.' She was wise to leave to others those sorrowful offices which were beyond her own power; exceeding wise, also, from that hour to her life's end, to remain in the shade, modestly bearing the honour which made her blessed among women. The mother of Zebedee's children, who also lingered late at the tomb, was gone home too, for as she was the mother of John it is exceedingly probable that John resided with her, and had taken the Virgin to her home: hence she was needed at home to act as hostess and assist her son, and thus she would be obeying the last wish of her dying Lord when he said 'Son, behold thy mother,' and explained his meaning by a look. All having thus departed, the two Marys were the sole watchers at the tomb of Christ at the time of the going down of the sun. They had work yet to do for his burial, and this called them away, but they stayed as long as they could – last to go and first to return.

This morning we shall with the women take up the somewhat unusual post of 'sitting over against the sepulchre'. I call it unusual, for as none remained save these two women, so few have preached upon our Redeemer's burial. Thousands of sermons have been delivered upon his death and resurrection, and in this I greatly rejoice, only wishing that there were thousands more; but still the burial of our Lord deserves a larger share of consideration than it generally obtains. 'He was crucified, dead, and buried,' says the creed, and therefore those who wrote that summary must have thought his burial an important truth; and so indeed it is. It was the natural sequence and seal of his death, and so was related to that which went before; it was the fit and suitable preparation for his rising again, and so stood in connection with that which followed after. Come, then, let us take our seat with the holy women 'over against the sepulchre', and sing:

> Rest, glorious Son of God: thy work is done,
> And all thy burdens borne;
> Rest on that stone till the third sun has brought
> Thine everlasting morn.
>
> How calmly in that tomb thou liest now,
> Thy rest how still and deep!
> O'er thee in love the Father rests: he gives
> To his beloved sleep.
>
> On Bethel pillow now thy head is laid,
> In Joseph's rock-hewn cell;
> Thy watchers are the angels of thy God
> They guard thy slumbers well.

1. Supposing ourselves to be sitting in the garden with our eyes fixed upon the great stone which formed the door of the tomb, we first of all *admire that he had a grave at all*. We wonder how that stone could hide him who is the brightness of his Father's glory; how the Life of all could lie among the dead; how he who holds creation in his strong

right hand could even for an hour be entombed. Admiring this, we would calmly reflect, first, upon *the testimony of his grave that he was really dead.* Those tender women could not have been mistaken, their eyes were too quick to suffer him to be buried alive, even if any one had wished to do so.

Of our Lord's actual death we have many proofs connected with his burial. When Joseph of Arimathaea went to Pilate and begged the body, the Roman ruler would not give it up till he was certified of his death. The centurion, a man under authority, careful in all that he did, certified that Jesus was dead. The soldier who served under the centurion had by a very conclusive test established the fact of his death beyond all doubt, for with a spear he pierced his side, and forthwith there came out blood and water. Pilate, who would not have given up the body of a condemned person unless he was sure that execution had taken place, registered the death and commanded the body to be delivered to Joseph. Both Joseph of Arimathaea and Nicodemus and all the friends who aided in the interment were beyond all question convinced that he was dead. They handled the lifeless frame, they wrapped it in the bands of fine linen, they placed the spices about the sacred flesh which they loved so well; they were sadly assured that their Lord was dead.

Even his enemies were quite certain that they had slain him: they never had a suspicion that possibly a little life remained in him, and that it could be revived, for their stern hate allowed no doubt to remain upon that point, they knew even to the satisfaction of their mistrustful malice that Jesus of Nazareth had died. Even when in their anxiety they went to Pilate, it was not that they might obtain stronger proofs of death, but to prevent the disciples from stealing his dead body and giving out that he had risen from the dead.

Yes, Jesus died, literally and actually died, and his body of flesh and bones was really laid in Joseph's grave. It was no phantom that was crucified, as certain heretics dreamed of old. We have not to look to a spectral atonement or to a visionary sacrifice, though some in our own times would reduce redemption to something shadowy and unsubstantial. Jesus was a real man, and truly tasted the bitter pangs of death; and therefore he in very deed lay in the sepulchre, motionless as the rock out of which it was hewn, shrouded in his winding-sheet.

Remember as you think of your Lord's death that the day will come, unless the second advent should intervene, in which you and I shall lie low among the dead, as once our Master did. Soon to this heart there will be left no pulsing life, to this eye no glance of observation, to this tongue no voice, to this ear no sensibility of sound. We naturally start from this, yet must it be. We shall certainly mingle with the dust we tread upon and feed the worm. But as we gaze on Jesus' tomb and assure ourselves that our great Lord and Master died each thought of dread is gone, and we no longer shudder: we feel that we can safely go where Christ has gone before.

Sitting down over against the sepulchre, after one has ruminated upon the wondrous fact that he who only hath immortality was numbered with the dead, the next subject which suggests itself is *the testimony of the grave to his union with us*. He had his grave hard by the city, and not on some lone mountain peak where foot of man could never tread. His grave was where it could be seen; it was a family grave which Joseph had no doubt prepared for himself and his household. Jesus was laid in a family vault where another had expected to lie. Where was Moses buried? No man knoweth of his sepulchre unto this day. But where Jesus was buried was well known to his friends. He was not caught away in a chariot of fire, nor was it said of him that God took him, but he was laid in the grave, 'as the manner of the Jews is to bury.' Jesus found his grave amongst the men he had redeemed. Hard by the common place of execution there was a garden, and in that garden they laid him in a tomb which was meant for others; so that our Lord's sepulchre stands, as it were, among our homes and gardens, and is one tomb among many.

Before me rises a picture. I see the cemetery, or sleeping place, of the saints, where each one rests on his lowly bed. They lie not alone, but like soldiers sleeping around their captain's pavilion, where he also spent the night, though he is up before them. The sepulchre of Jesus is the central grave of God's acre; it is empty now, but his saints lie buried all around that cave in the rock, gathered in ranks around their dear Redeemer's resting-place. Surely it robs the grave of its ancient terror when we think that Jesus slept in one of the chambers of the great dormitory of the sons of men.

Very much might be said about the tomb in which Jesus lay. It was a *new* tomb, wherein no remains had been previously laid, and thus if he came forth from it there would be no suspicion that another had arisen, nor could it be imagined that he rose through touching some old prophet's bones, as he did who was laid in Elisha's grave. As he was born of a virgin mother, so was he buried in a virgin tomb, wherein never man had lain. It was a *rocky* tomb, and therefore nobody could dig into it by night, or tunnel through the earth. It was a *borrowed* tomb; so poor was Jesus that he owed a grave to charity; but that tomb was spontaneously offered, so rich was he in the love of hearts which he had won. That tomb he returned to Joseph, honoured unspeakably by his temporary sojourn therein. I know not whether Joseph ever used it for any of his house; but I see no reason why he should not have done so. Certainly, our Lord when he borrows always makes prompt repayment, and gives a bonus over: he filled Simon's boat with fish when he used it for a pulpit, and he sanctified the rocky cell wherein he had lodged, and left it perfumed for the next who should sleep therein.

We, too, expect, unless special circumstances should intervene, that these bodies of ours will lie in their narrow beds beneath the greensward, and slumber till the resurrection. Nor need we be afraid of the tomb, for Jesus has been there. Sitting over against his sepulchre we grow brave, and are ready, like knights of the holy sepulchre, to hurl defiance at death. At times we almost long for evening to undress that we may rest with God, in the chamber where he giveth to his beloved sleep.

Now, note that our Lord's tomb was in a garden; for this is typically *the testimony of his grave to the hope of better things*. Just a little beyond the garden wall you would see a little knoll, of grim name and character, the Tyburn of Jerusalem, Golgotha, the place of a skull, and there stood the cross. That rising ground was given up to horror and barrenness; but around the actual tomb of our Saviour there grew herbs and plants and flowers. A spiritual garden still blooms around his tomb; the wilderness and the solitary place are glad for him, and the desert rejoices and blossoms as the rose. He hath made another Paradise for us, and he himself is the sweetest flower therein. The first Adam sinned in a garden and spoiled our nature; the second Adam slept in a garden and restored our loss. The Saviour buried in the earth hath removed the curse from the soil; henceforth blessed is the ground for his sake. He died for us that we ourselves might become in heart and life fruitful gardens of the Lord. Let but his tomb, and all the facts which surround it, have due influence upon the minds of men, and this poor blighted earth shall again yield her increase: instead of the thorn shall come up the fir tree, and instead of the brier shall come up the myrtle tree, and it shall be to the Lord for a name.

Sitting over against the sepulchre perhaps the best thought of all is that now it is empty and *so bears testimony to our resurrection*. It must have made the two Marys weep, when before they left the grave they saw it filled with so beloved a treasure, so surely dead; they ought to have rejoiced to find it empty when they returned, but they knew not as yet the angel's message, 'He is not here, for he is risen.' Our Christ is not dead now; he ever liveth to make intercession for us. He could not be holden by the bands of death. There was nothing corruptible about him, and therefore his body has left the abode of decay to live in newness of life. The sepulchre is spoiled and the spoiler has gone up to glory, leading captivity captive. As you sit over against the sepulchre let your hearts be comforted concerning death, whose sting is gone for ever. There shall be a resurrection. Be ye sure of this, for if the dead rise not then is Christ not risen; but the Lord is risen indeed, and his rising necessitates that all who are in him should rise as he has done.

Yet another thought comes to me – Can I follow Christ as fully as these two women did? That is to say, can

I still cling to him though to sense and reason his cause should seem dead and laid in a rocky sepulchre? Can I like Joseph and Magdalene be a disciple of a dead Christ? Could I follow him even at his lowest point? I want to apply this practically. Times have come upon the Christian church when truth seems to be fallen in the streets, and the kingdom of Christ is in apparent peril. Just now the Lord Jesus is betrayed by not a few of his professed ministers. He is being crucified afresh in the perpetual attacks of scepticism against his blessed gospel; and it may be things may wax worse and worse. This is not the first occasion when it has been so, for at various times in the history of the church of God his enemies have exulted, and cried out that the gospel of past ages was exploded, and might be reckoned as dead and buried. For one I mean to sit over against the very sepulchre of truth. I am a disciple of the old-fashioned doctrine as much when it is covered with obloquy and rebuke as when it shall again display its power, as it surely shall. Sceptics may seem to take truth and bind it, and scourge it, and crucify it, and say that it is dead, and they may endeavour to bury it in scorn, but the Lord has many a Joseph and a Nicodemus who will see honour done even to the body of truth, and will wrap the despised creed in sweet spices, and hide it away in their hearts. They may, perhaps, be half afraid that it is really dead, as the wise men assert, yet it is precious to their souls, and they will come forth right gladly to espouse its cause, and to confess that they are its disciples. We will sit down in sorrow but not in despair, and watch until the stone is rolled away, and Christ in his truth shall live again, and be openly triumphant. We shall see a divine interposition and shall cease to fear; while they who stand armed to prevent the resurrection of the grand old doctrine shall quake and become as dead men, because the gospel's everlasting life has been vindicated, and they are made to quail before the brightness of its glory.

This, then, is our first meditation: we admire that Jesus ever had a grave, and we sit in wonder over against the sepulchre.

2. Secondly, sitting here, *we rejoice in the honours of his burial.* The burial of Christ was, under some aspects of it, the lowest step of his humiliation: he must not merely for a moment die, but he must be buried awhile in the heart of the earth. On the other hand, under other aspects our Lord's burial was the first step of his glory: it was a turning-point in his great career, as we shall hope to show you. Our Lord's body was given up by Pilate to Joseph, and he went with authority to receive it from those who were appointed to see him take it down. I yesterday had a glimpse at a work of art by one of our own Lambeth neighbours, exhibited by Mr. Doulton; it is a fine piece of work in terracotta, representing the taking down of Christ from the cross. I could have wished to have studied it more at leisure, but a mere glimpse has charmed me. The artist represents a Roman soldier at the top of the cross taking down the parchment upon which the accusation was written; he is rolling it up to put it away for ever. I thought of the taking away of the handwriting which was against *him*, even as he had taken away that which was against *us*. The Roman soldier by authority is thus represented as removing the charge which was once nailed over the ever blessed head; there is no accusation against him now: he died, and the law is satisfied, it can no longer accuse the man who has endured its penalty. Another soldier is represented with

a pair of pincers drawing out one of the big nails from the hands; the sacred body is free now, law has no further claims upon it, and withdraws its nails. A disciple, not a soldier, has mounted a ladder on the other side, and with a pair of scissors is cutting away the crown of thorns; and I think the artist did well to represent his doing so, for henceforth it is our delight to remove all shame from the name of Jesus, and to crown him in another fashion. Then the artist has represented certain of his disciples as gently taking hold of the body as it is gradually being unloosed by the soldiers, while Joseph of Arimathaea stands there with his long linen sheet ready to receive him. Jars of precious myrrh and spices are standing there, and the women ready to open the lids and to place the spices around the holy flesh.

Every part of the design is significant and instructive, and the artist deserves great praise for it: it brought before my mind the descent from the cross with greater vividness than any painting I have ever seen. The nails are all extracted, he is held no longer to the cross, the body is taken down, no longer to be spit upon, and despised, and rejected, but tenderly handled by his friends; for all and everything that has to do with shame, and suffering, and paying of penalty is ended once for all. What became of the cross of wood? You find in Scripture no further mention of it. The legends concerning it are all false upon the face of them. The cross is gone for ever; neither gibbet, nor nail, nor spear, nor thorny crown can be found; there is no further use for them. Jesus our Lord has gone to his glory; for by his one sacrifice he hath secured the salvation of his own.

But now as to his burial. Beloved, there were many honourable circumstances about it. Its first effect was *the development of timid minds.* Joseph of Arimathaea occupied a high post as an honourable councillor, but he was a secret disciple. Nicodemus, too, was a ruler of the Jews, and though he had spoken a word for the Master now and then, as probably Joseph had done (for we are told that he had not consented to their counsel and deed), yet he had never come out boldly till now. He came to Jesus by night aforetime, but he came by daylight now. At the worst estate of the Saviour's cause we should have thought that these two men would remain concealed, but they did not. Now that the case seemed desperate, they show their faith in Jesus and pluck up courage to honour their Lord. Lambs become lions when the Lamb is slain. Joseph went boldly in unto Pilate and begged the body of Jesus. For a dead Christ he risks his position, and even his life, for he is asking the body of a reputed traitor, and may himself be put to death by Pilate; or else the members of the Sanhedrin may be enraged at him, and bind themselves with an oath that they will slay him for paying honour to the Nazarene, whom they called 'that deceiver'. Joseph can venture everything for Jesus, even though he knows him to be dead.

Equally brave is Nicodemus; for publicly at the foot of the cross he stands with his hundred pounds weight of spices, caring nothing for any who may report the deed. I cheerfully hope, dear brethren, that one result of the ferocious attacks made upon the gospel at this time will be that a great number of quiet and retiring spirits will be roused to energy and courage. Such works of evil might move the very stones to cry out. While, perhaps, some who have spoken well in other days and have usually done the battling may be downcast and quiet, these who have kept in the rear rank, and have only in secret followed Jesus, will be brought to the front, and we shall see men of substance and of position avowing their Lord. Joseph and Nicodemus both illustrate the dreadful truth that it is hard for them that have riches to enter into the kingdom of God; but they also show us that when they do enter they frequently excel. If they come last they remain to the last. If cowards when others are heroes, they can also be heroes when even apostles are cowards. Each man has his turn, and so while the fishermen-apostles were hiding away, the wealthy non-committal brethren came to the front. Though bred in luxury, they bore the brunt of the storm, and avowed the cause whose leader lay dead. Brave are the hearts which stand up for Jesus in his burial. 'Sitting over against the sepulchre,' we draw comfort from the sight of the friends who honoured the Lord in his death.

I like to remember that the burial of the Lord *displayed the union of loving hearts.* The tomb became the meeting-place of the old disciples and the new, of those who had long consorted with the Master, and those who had but newly avowed him. Magdalene and Mary had been with the Lord for years, and had ministered to him of their substance; but Joseph of Arimathaea, as far as his public avowal of Christ is concerned, was, like Nicodemus, a new disciple: old and new followers united in the deed of love, and laid their Master in the tomb. A common sorrow and a common love unite us wondrously. When our great Master's cause is under a cloud and his name blasphemed it is pleasant to see the young men battling with the foe and aiding their fathers in the stern struggle. Magdalene with her penitent love, and Mary with her deep attachment to her Lord, join with the rabbi and the counsellor who now begin to prove that they intensely love the Man of

Nazareth. That small society, that little working meeting, which gathered around our Master's body, was a type of the whole Christian church. When once aroused, believers forget all differences and degrees of spiritual condition, and each one is eager to do his part to honour his Lord.

Mark, too, that the Saviour's death *brought out abundant liberality*. The spices, one hundred pounds in weight, and the fine linen, were furnished by the men; and then the holy women prepared the liquid spices with which to carry out what they might have called his great funeral, when they would more completely wrap the body in odoriferous spices as the manner of the Jews was to bury. There was much of honour intended by all that they brought. A very thoughtful writer observes that the clothes in which our Lord was wrapped are not called grave-clothes, but linen clothes, and that the emphasis would seem to be put upon their being linen; and he reminds us that when we read of the garments of the priests in the Book of the Law we find that every garment must be of linen. Our Lord's priesthood is, therefore, suggested by the sole use of linen for his death robes. The Apostle and High Priest of our profession in his tomb slept in pure white linen, even as now today he represents himself to his servants as clothed with a garment down to the foot. Even after death he acted as a priest, and poured out a libation of blood and water; and it was, therefore, meet that in the grave he should still wear priestly garments.

'He made his grave with the wicked' – there was his shame; 'but with the rich in his death' – there was his honour. He was put to death by rough soldiery, but he was laid in his grave by tender women. Persons of honourable estate helped gently to receive, and reverentially to place in its position his dear and sacred frame; and then, as if to do him honour, though they meant it not, his tomb must not be left unsentinelled, and Caesar lends his guards to watch the couch of the Prince of Peace. Like a king he slumbers, till as the King of kings he wakes at daybreak.

To my mind it is very pleasant to see all this honour come to our Lord when he is in his worst estate – dead and buried. Will we not also honour our Lord when others despise him? Will we not cleave to him, come what may? If the church were all but extirpated, if every voice should go over to the enemy, if a great stone of philosophic reasoning were rolled at the door of truth, and it should seem no longer possible for argument to remove it, yet would we wait till the gospel should rise again to confound its foes. We will not be afraid, but keep our position; we will stand still and see the salvation of God, or 'sitting over against the sepulchre', we will watch for the Lord's coming. Let the worst come to the worst we would sooner serve Christ while he is conceived to be dead than all the philosophers that ever lived when in their prime. Even if fools should dance over the grave of Christianity there shall remain at least a few who will weep over it, and brushing away their tears from their eyes expect to see it revive, and put forth all its ancient strength.

3. I must now pass to a third point. While sitting over against the sepulchre *we observe that his enemies were not at rest*. They had their own way, but they were not content; they had taken the Saviour, and with wicked hands they had crucified and slain him; but they were not satisfied. They were the most uneasy people in the world, though they had gained their point. It was their Sabbath day, and it was a high day, that Sabbath of Sabbaths, the Sabbath of the Passover. They kept a preparation for it and had been very

careful not to go into the place called the pavement, lest they should defile themselves – sweet creatures! And now have they not gained all they wanted? They have killed Jesus and buried him: are they not happy? No: and what is more, their humiliation had begun – they were doomed to belie their own favourite profession. What was that profession? Their boast of rigid Sabbath-keeping was its chief point, and they were perpetually charging our blessed Lord with Sabbath-breaking, for healing the sick, and even because his disciples rubbed a few ears of wheat between their hands, when they were hungry on the Sabbath day.

Brethren, look at these men and laugh at their hypocrisy. It is the Sabbath-day, and they come to Pilate, holding counsel on the Sabbath with a heathen! They tell him that they are afraid that Jesus' body will be spirited away, and he says, 'Ye have a watch; go your way, make it as sure as you can'; and they go and seal the stone on the Sabbath. O ye hypocritical Pharisees, here was an awful breaking of your Sabbath by your own selves! According to their superstitious tradition the rubbing ears of wheat between the hands was a kind of threshing, and therefore it was a breach of the law; surely, by the same reasoning the burning of a candle to melt the wax must have been similar to the lighting of a furnace, and the melting of wax must have been a kind of foundry work, like that of the smith who pours metal into a mould; for in such a ridiculous fashion their rabbis interpreted the smallest acts. But they had to seal the stone and break their own absurd laws to satisfy their restless malice. One is pleased to see either Pharisees or Sadducees made to overturn their own professions and lay bare their hypocrisy. Modern-thought gentlemen will, ere long, be forced to the same humiliation.

Next, they had to retract their own accusation against our Lord. They charged Jesus with having said, 'Destroy this temple, and I will build it in three days,' pretending that he referred to the temple upon Zion. Now they come to Pilate and tell him, 'This deceiver said, after three days I will rise again.' Oh, ye knaves, that is your new version, is it? Ye put the man to death for quite another rendering! Now you understand the dark saying? Yes, ye deceivers, and ye understood it before; but now ye must eat your leek, and swallow your own words. Truly, he scorneth the scorners, and poureth contempt upon his enemies. And now see how these kill-Christs betray their own fears. He is dead, but they are afraid of him! He is dead, but they cannot shake off the dread that he will vanquish them yet. They are full of agitation and alarm.

Nor was this all, they were to be made witnesses for God, to sign certificates of the death and resurrection of his Anointed. In order that there might be no doubt about the resurrection at all, there must be a seal, and they must go and set it; there must be a guard, and they must see it mustered. The disciples need not trouble about certifying that Jesus is in the grave; these Jews will do it, and set their own great seal to the evidence. These proud ones are sent to do drudges' work in Christ's kitchen, to wait upon a dead Christ, and to protect the body which they had slain. The lie which they told afterwards crowned their shame: they bribed the soldiers to say that his disciples stole him away while they slept; and this was a transparent falsehood; for if the soldiers were asleep how could they know what was done? We cannot conceive of an instance in which men were more completely made to contradict and convict themselves.

That Sabbath was a high day, but it was no Sabbath to them, nor would the overthrow of the gospel be any rest of soul to its opponents. If ever we should live to see the truth pushed into a corner, and the blessed cause of Christ fastened up as with rationalistic nails, and its very heart pierced by a critic's spear; yet, mark you, even in the darkest night that can ever try our faith, the adversaries of the gospel will still be in alarm lest it should rise again. The old truth has a wonderful habit of leaping up from every fall as strong as ever. In Dr Doddridge's days men had pretty nearly buried the gospel. Socinianism was taught in many if not most dissenting pulpits, and the same was true of the Church of England: the liberal thinkers dreamed that they had won the victory and extinguished evangelical teaching; but their shouting came a little too soon. They said, 'We shall hear no more of this miserable justification by faith, and regeneration by the Holy Ghost.' They laid the gospel in a tomb cut out in the cold rock of Unitarianism, and they set the seal of their learning upon the great stone of doubt which shut in the gospel. There it was to lie for ever; but God meant otherwise. There was a pot-boy over in Gloucester called George Whitefield, and there was a young student who had lately gone to Oxford called John Wesley, and these two passed by the grave of the gospel and beheld a strange sight, which they began to tell; and as they told it, the sods of unbelief and the stones of learned criticism began to move, and the truth which had been buried started up with Pentecostal power. Aha! ye adversaries, how greatly had ye deceived yourselves! Within a few months all over England the work of the devil and his ministers was broken to pieces, as when a tower is split by lightning, or the thick darkness scattered by the rising sun. The weight of ignorance and unbelief fled before the bright day of the gospel, though that gospel was for the most part proclaimed by unlettered men. The thing which has been is the thing which shall be. History repeats itself.

O generation of modern thinkers, you will have to eat your own words, and disprove your own assertions. You will have to confute each other and yourselves, even as the Moabites and Elamites slew each other. It may even happen that your infidelities will work themselves out into practical evil of which you will be the victims. You may bring about a repetition of the French Revolution of 1789, with more than all its bloodshed, and who will wonder. You, some of you calling yourselves ministers of God, with your insinuations of doubt, your denials of future punishment, your insults of the gospel, your ingenious speeches against the Bible, are shaking the very foundation of society. I impeach you as the worst enemies of mankind. In effect you proclaim to men that they may sin as they like, for there is no hell, or if there be, it is but a little one: thus you publish a gospel of licentiousness, and you may one day rue the result. You may live to see a reign of terror of your own creating, but even if you do, the gospel of Jesus will come forth from all the filth you have heaped upon it, for the holy gospel will live as Christ lives, and its enemies shall never cease to be in fear. Your harsh speeches against those who preach the gospel, your bitterness and your sneers of contempt, all show that you know better than you say, and are afraid of the very Christ whom you kill. We who cleave to the glorious gospel will abide in peace, come what may, but you will not.

4. And now our last thought is that while these enemies of Christ were in fear and trembling *we note that his followers were resting.* It was the seventh day, and therefore they ceased from labour. The Marys waited, and Joseph and Nicodemus refrained from visiting the tomb; they obediently observed the Sabbath rest. I am not sure that they had faith enough to feel very happy, but they evidently did expect something, and anxiously awaited the third day. They had enough of the comfort of hope to remain quiet on the seventh day.

Now, beloved, sitting over against the sepulchre while Christ lies in it, my first thought about it is, *I will rest, for he rests.* What a wonderful stillness there was about our Lord in that rocky grave. He had been daily thronged by thousands: even when he ate bread they disturbed him. He scarce could have a moment's stillness in life; but now how quiet is his bed! Not a sound is heard. The great stone shuts out all noise, and the body is at peace. Well, if he rests, I may. If for a while the Lord seems to suspend his energies, his servants may cry unto him, but they may not fret. He knows best when to sleep and when to wake.

As I see the Christ resting in the grave, my next thought is, *he has the power to come forth again.* Some few months ago I tried to show you that when the disciples were alarmed because Jesus was asleep they were in error, for his sleep was the token of their security. When I see a captain on board ship pacing anxiously up and down the deck, I may fear that danger is suspected; but when the captain turns into his cabin, then I may be sure that all is right, and there is no reason why I should not turn in too. So if our blessed Lord should ever suffer his cause to droop, and if he should give no marvellous manifestations of his power, we need not doubt his power; let us keep our Sabbath, pray to him, and work for him, for these are duties of the holy day of rest; but do not let us fret and worry, for his time to work will come.

The rest of the Christian lies in believing in Christ under all circumstances. Go in for this, beloved. Believe in him in the manger, when his cause is young and weak. Believe in him in the streets, when the populace applaud him, for he deserves their loudest acclamations. Believe in him when they take him to the brow of the hill to cast him headlong, he is just as worthy as when they cry 'Hosanna.' Believe in him when he is in an agony, and believe in him when he is on the cross; and if ever it should seem to you that his cause must die out, believe in him still. Christ's gospel in any circumstances deserves our fullest trust. That gospel which has saved your souls, that gospel which ye have received, and which has been sealed upon your hearts by the Holy Ghost, stand fast in it, come what may, and through faith peace and quiet shall pervade your souls.

Once more, it will be well if we can obtain peace by having fellowship with our Lord in his burial. Die with him, and be buried with him; there is nothing like it. I desire for my soul while she lives in the Lord that, as to the world and all its wisdom, I may be as a dead man. When accused of having no power of thought, and no originality of teaching, I am content to own the charge, for my soul desires to be dead to all but that which is revealed and taught by the Lord Jesus. I would lie in the rocky tomb of the everlasting truth, not creating thought, but giving myself up to God's thoughts. But, brethren, if we are ever to lie in that tomb, we must be wrapped about with the fine linen of holiness: these are the shrouds of a man who is dead to sin. All about us must be the spices, the myrrh, and aloes of preserving grace, that being dead with Christ we may see no corruption, but may show that death to be only another form of the new life which we have received in him. When the world goes by, let it know concerning our heart's desire and ambition, that they are all buried with Christ, and it is written on the memorial of our spiritual grave, 'Here he lies'; as far as this world's sin, and pleasure, and self-seeking, and wisdom are concerned, 'Here he lies buried with his Master.'

Know, you who are not converted, that the way of salvation is by believing in Christ, or trusting in him, and if you do so trust you shall never be confounded, world without end, for he that trusteth Christ, and believeth in him even as a little child, the same shall enter into his kingdom, and he that will follow him, even down to his grave, shall be with him in his glory, and shall see his triumphs for ever and ever. Amen.

6

Christ's Manifestation to Mary Magdalene[1]

Jesus saith unto her, 'Touch me not; for I am not yet ascended to my Father: but go to my brethren, and say unto them, I ascend unto my Father, and your Father; and to my God, and your God'.
John 20:17

This was the first appearance of our Lord Jesus Christ after his resurrection. In sundry places and at diverse times, during the ensuing forty days, he appeared to different disciples, showing himself openly to them when they were assembled for worship, and at other seasons; but this was the first occasion of his being seen by any of his followers after he had risen from the dead. The

---

1. Preached on a Sunday evening in the summer of 1859 in New Park Street Chapel, Southwark.

whole incident is full of consolation, and we, who are poor weary pilgrims through this earthly wilderness, need some words of comfort every now and then to cheer us on the road. May the Holy Spirit sweetly assist us in meditating now upon the things of Christ, and may our hearts burn within us as he speaks to us by the way!

1. First, it is peculiarly encouraging to remember that the first person to whom our Lord Jesus Christ appeared after his resurrection was Mary Magdalene. Mark expressly says, 'Now when Jesus was risen early the first day of the week, he appeared first to Mary Magdalene, out of whom he had cast seven devils.' Romanists will have it that Jesus Christ first of all appeared to the Virgin Mary, his mother, and they have invented some curious stories in order to give her this peculiar honour. This shows that, in their opinion, there was a special favour conferred upon the person who first beheld the risen Saviour; and I need not say that their assertion that it was the Virgin Mary is only just another instance of their common practice of perverting the truth. Undoubtedly, Mary Magdalene was the first person who saw the Saviour after his resurrection; at least, if the Roman guards saw him when they shook, and became as dead men through fear of the angel who rolled away the stone from the sepulchre, they were not Christ's disciples; so I mean that Mary Magdalene was the first of his faithful followers who had the honour of seeing him after he rose from the dead.

It was a woman, then, who first beheld the risen Saviour. It was a woman who was first in the transgression; it had, therefore, to be a woman who should first behold Jesus Christ when he rose from the grave. If there be – and there certainly is some degree of opprobrium connected with womanhood, because Eve first of all touched the forbidden fruit, there is a far greater degree of glory now connected with it, because Mary Magdalene first of all beheld the Saviour after his rising from the tomb.

Not only was it a woman to whom Christ first manifested himself after his resurrection, but it was a woman out of whom he had cast seven devils. I am inclined to think that there were other devils in Mary Magdalene beside those that made her a demoniac. Luther used to say of her, 'So many devils, so many sins.' She had been first a sinner, then she became a demoniac, and afterwards Christ changed her into a saint. How strange it was that Jesus should appear first to her! What, give the highest honour to her who had the most of sin! Sweet thought! Then, if – 'I the chief of sinners am' – if I have an interest in the blood of Christ there is no reason why I should not climb to the greatest heights of fellowship, and enjoy the best of the good things which the Lord hath prepared for them that love him. When Jesus takes a sinner to himself, his pardon is so complete, so totally does God, for Christ's sake, overlook all previous sin, that although he may not be as great a saint as the very chief of the apostles, who did most grievously rebel, so that he only obtained mercy because he did it ignorantly in unbelief, he may be the most highly-favoured of the servants of the Lord, and may have very special revelations made to him. The experience of Mary Magdalene should be a great source of comfort to you who, after years of sin, have lately found the Saviour. Think not that those years that you spent in folly, though they must ever make you weep, will be the means of robbing you of fellowship with him. Oh, no! he will restore to you the years that the locusts have eaten, and he will not take away from you the pleasure of enjoying the bliss of God on earth, and certainly he will not diminish your glorious happiness when you shall stand before his throne above.

In thinking over this subject, I have come to the conclusion that Mary Magdalene was selected to see Christ first because she loved him most. John loved Jesus much, but Mary loved him more. John looked into the empty sepulchre, and then went away home; but Mary stood there, and wept, until her risen Lord appeared to her. Love, you know, is a keen-eyed grace. People usually say that love is blind. In one sense, the saying is true; but, in another sense, there never were such good eyes anywhere else as those which love carries in her head. Love will look for Jesus, and discover him where none else can. If I set the unloving to read a chapter in the Bible, they will find no Saviour there; but if I ask the gracious Robert Hawker to read that same portion of Scripture, he finds in it the name of Jesus from beginning to end. If I beg one, who is simply a critical scholar, to study a Psalm, he sees no Messiah there; but if I set an enthusiastic lover of the Saviour to read it, he sees him, if not in every verse, still here and there he has glimpses of his glory.

If you want to see Jesus, and to have sweet revelations of his glory, you must love him. I must add to that remark, that you must weep for him much, you must seek him diligently, seek him in the darkness and the twilight, seek him when the sun has risen, seek him at the sepulchre before the stone is rolled away; you must seek him when you behold that the stone is gone; you must seek him in the hollow tomb; you must seek him in the garden; you must seek him in life; you must seek him in death; and then, the more diligent you are in seeking, the greater is the probability that Christ will manifest himself to you, and that you shall rejoice in finding him. Mary Magdalene was one of those who went forth bearing precious seed; she went forth weeping, but she returned to the disciples rejoicing, bringing her sheaves with her, for she had a joyous message for them. She had sown in tears when she went to seek her Lord, but she wept with joy when she found him in the garden. Happy was that woman who found Jesus, and who believed; truly she might rejoice in him, for she was highly favoured among women.

You see, then, that there is much sweetness, far more than I can tell you, in the thought that Mary Magdalene was the first person who was chosen to see the Lord Jesus Christ after his resurrection.

2. Secondly, we will notice *some reasons for the prohibition given in the text.* Why was it that Jesus said to Mary, 'Touch me not'? And why was it that he gave this very strange reason for the prohibition, 'for I am not yet ascended to my Father'?

There seems to me to be great comfort in this message; I know it has comforted me, so I think I understand it aright. When Mary Magdalene had recognized her risen Redeemer, and had called him 'Rabboni, that is to say, Master,' her next impulse was to cast herself upon him, and embrace him. But Jesus said to her, 'No; embrace me not' − for that is the real meaning of the word − 'I have something for you to do for me, so I cannot allow you to stop to manifest your affection; there will be plenty of time to do that another day. I want to send you to my disciples at once with a message; therefore, cling not to me. The strengthening of my disciples is preferable even to the embracing of your Lord. Cling not to me, for I am not yet ascended.' It strikes me that Mary was half afraid that her Master would go away directly; and she thought, 'That is my Master, for I know his voice; but I fear that he will vanish; the Spirit of God will take him away.' She thought concerning Christ just as Obadiah did concerning Elijah. When Obadiah found the prophet, Elijah said to him, 'Go, tell thy lord, Behold, Elijah is here.' 'And he said, What have I sinned, that thou wouldest deliver thy servant into the hand of Ahab, to slay me? As the Lord thy God liveth, there is no nation or kingdom, whither my lord hath not sent to seek thee: and when they said, He is not there; he took an oath of the kingdom and nation, that they found thee not. And now thou sayest, Go, tell thy lord, Behold, Elijah is here. And it shall come to pass, as soon as I am gone from thee, that the Spirit of the Lord shall carry thee whither I know not; and so when I come and tell Ahab, and he cannot find thee, he shall slay me.' Obadiah expected that Elijah would be spirited away, and Mary thought the same concerning Christ; so she said to herself, 'I will hold him fast. This may be my only opportunity; so I will not let him go.' But Jesus said, 'I am not going away; I shall be here a little while longer; there will be time enough for embraces yet. The first thing I want you to do is to go to my disciples, and tell them that I have risen from the grave, and that I am about to ascend to heaven.'

If you ask, 'Why did Jesus speak thus to Mary Magdalene?', I think it is not difficult to explain the reason. Let me suppose that one of you has said, 'I will have an hour for quiet meditation; I will cast myself upon my knees; I will open the Word of God; I will seek the Spirit to rest upon me; and I will hope that I shall be able to see Jesus, and to clasp him in my arms.' Just as you have formed this resolve, a friend calls, and says that he has an important engagement for you to fulfil. Perhaps he wants you to attend a prayer-meeting, or to visit the sick, or to see some enquirer, or to do something for the Lord's cause; and you say, 'There now; I expected to have had this evening for contemplation. Oh, I wish I had not so much to do with the church, for it robs me of my quiet hours! I love those sweet seasons of retirement when I can embrace the Saviour, and clasp him to my heart. Why is it that I am to go out and feed the flock, and not find time for fellowship and communion so long and frequent as I desire?' Whenever you feel inclined to talk like that, think that you hear your Master saying to you, 'Embrace me not; there will be time in heaven for that. Go thou to my brethren, and carry to them some words of consolation; for while it is sweet for thee to embrace me, it is sweeter to me for thee to go and embrace my poor brother, and show him the way into my kingdom.'

God forbid that we should say one word against the high joys of contemplation! It is a blessed employment; but, sometimes, work is better than worship; or rather, work is worship in its best form. Sometimes, it is a higher service to go to see the sick than to be at home on your knees. Sometimes, it is a more devout way of serving God to be busy for the church, even in what seem to be temporal matters, than to be seated at home, like Mary of old, at the feet of the Saviour, listening to his words, but doing nothing for his cause. I believe Martha is at times a great deal more than Mary. If Mary had always sat at the Saviour's feet, she would have deserved no commendation. It was well that she sat there then, for it was a proper occasion; but if she had sat there always, and left Martha to attend to the serving alone, then it would have been an abuse of her privileges. There are times when the Master must say, 'Embrace me not; but go to my brethren, and tell them that I ascend to my Father, and your Father; and to my God, and your God.'

3. Now, having noticed these two portions of our text, which I think are full of comfort, if not to you, they certainly have been to me, I will now endeavour to dilate upon *the message of our Lord to Mary Magdalene.* Jesus said to her, 'Go to my brethren.' It is a remarkable fact that *the higher Jesus Christ gets in glory, the more sweet are his expressions of love.* You know that, before his death, he said to his disciples: 'Henceforth I call you not servants; for the servant knoweth not what his lord doeth: but I have called you friends; for all things that I have heard of my Father I have made known unto you.' Yet now that he had risen from the dead, he called them by a still higher name. Possibly, some of them thought, 'If he should rise from the dead, he will be ashamed of us poor fishermen. He called us "friends" when he was in his poverty; will he not return to that word "servants" when he rises in majesty from the tomb?' No; when he had risen in dignity, it was just the reverse. The higher his dignity, the lower his condescension. 'Go to my *brethren.'*

There is another thing to be noted about that sweet word 'brethren' as Christ then used it, for his disciples were never in a more sinful condition than they were at that time; or, rather, they had never so grossly sinned as they had done a little before the Saviour's resurrection. They were with him every day; they were, all of them, in a measure faithful, and never forsook their Master, and never denied him, till he came to die. Yet, all the time they were true and faithful, he called them friends. You would have thought that, when three of them slept in the garden during his awful agony, when all forsook him and fled, and when Peter especially denied him, the Saviour would have said, 'I called you friends when you were faithful, I will now see whether I can stretch a point, even to call you servants.' But we see that, the blacker was their sin, the stronger was his love; the more defiled they were, the more sweetly did he talk to them. He said to them, in deeds though not in words, 'Henceforth, I call you not friends, for a mere friend is no relation; but I call you brethren, for my Father is your Father, and my God is your God.'

Carry those two sweet thoughts away with you, for sweet indeed they will be to you if the Holy Spirit shall teach you the full meaning of them – that the higher the Saviour gets, the more free is he in the expression of his love; and that other thought, that the farther the disciples ran away from their Master, the more lovingly did he call them back again. This is marvellous and strange, but it is nevertheless true; who cannot derive comfort from such thoughts as these? I know, ye feeble followers of Jesus, ye have sometimes thought that he loved his people when he was on earth, but that now he reigns exalted on high, he has forgotten such of them as you are; but be ye assured that, inasmuch as he has reached the summit of his glory, he doth now manifest the summit of his love. The more he is exalted, the more doth he manifest himself.

Possibly, some of you are thinking that you have so greatly sinned that you cannot expect him to love you. If so, you can appropriate this thought that *the sweetest promises in the Bible are for the very people who deserve them the least*. There are promises for those who follow close to their Saviour, and very sweet ones, too; but some of the tenderest promises in the Word of God are for those who have wandered furthest away from him. Take, for instance, this gracious message, 'Return, thou backsliding Israel, saith the Lord; and I will not cause mine anger to fall upon you: for I am merciful, saith the Lord, and I will not keep anger for ever. Only acknowledge thine iniquity, that thou hast transgressed against the Lord thy God, and hast scattered thy ways to the strangers under every green tree, and ye have not obeyed my voice, saith the Lord. Turn, O backsliding children, saith the Lord; for I am married unto you: and I will take you one of a city, and two of a family, and I will bring you to Zion.' Blessed Jesus, when we should have thought that our sins would cause thee to speak most harshly against us, we find that thou hast the softest words for those who have most erred; that our sins, which must make thee angry, seem also to make thee invite us back again with sweeter words than thou dost use to those who have not grieved thee as much as we have done.

Note again, *every time our Lord Jesus Christ says anything to his brethren, it is something that requires faith on their part.* Why did he not say, 'Go and tell my brethren that I have risen from the grave'! Because they did not need any faith for that. He had risen; that was a fact that they could discover by their eyesight, and some of them by their touch. 'No,' says he, 'I will make large drafts upon my people's faith. Go and tell them that I am about to ascend to my Father; that is something great for them to believe.' Do you know, Christian friends, that the more you have of the manifest presence of Christ, the more faith you require! Have you not often asked to have a promise brought home to your heart by the special influences of the Spirit? Now, recollect, the more promises you have, the more faith you will require. The words of Christ demand faith on our part. A manifestation from Christ is as truly a demand upon our faith as when he hides his face from us. When he hides his face, he requires us still to believe in him even when he says nothing; but when he speaks, he requires us to believe something that he says. The more manifestations Christ grants to you, the more is your need of faith.

'I ascend unto my Father, and your Father; and to my God, and your God.' Luther was right when he said that all the pith of divinity lay in the pronouns. '*My* Father and *your* Father.' 'He is "my Father" by eternal generation. I was begotten of my Father before any of the worlds were made. He is "your Father" by regeneration. He hath begotten you again unto a lively hope by the resurrection of Jesus Christ from the dead. He is "my Father" as I am the Head of the Church − I call him "Father" in my Christhood, as God and man; and as I am your Representative, and you are all gathered up in me, he is your Father, too: my Father, and your Father.'

How sweet is the word 'Father' in such a connection! He is our Father because he has the deepest love to protect us; and if we doubt whether his power is equal to his love, let us notice what Jesus next says, 'I ascend to my God, and your God.' And inasmuch as God is omnipotent, and the Father is love, you have all the love you need, and all the power equal to that love. It seems sweet to hear Christ calling his Father his God. As he was a man, the Father was his God; as he was Christ, the God-man, the Father was God over him; and speaking as a man, he could say, 'My Father is greater than I,' God the Father being greater than the Mediator, who said, in effect, 'As man, I worship him even as you worship him; as man, I look up to him as my

Father the same as you do. He is my Father as he is your Father.'

I have only to make one other remark, *how beautifully the Saviour refers to the believer's union with himself!* The whole Bible, when it is rightly understood, points to the believer's union with Christ, and this sweet verse is full of that blessed truth. Christ and his people have united interests. When Christ calls God his Father, we may call God '*our* Father' too. In his inheritance we have a joint interest; he is Heir of all things, and we are joint-heirs with him. In relationship, Christ and his people are closely united. His brethren are our brethren; his Father is our Father. Even in service, as Christ was man, as he was the Servant of God for our sakes, so the Master whom he served is the Master whom we serve, and we together take the same service upon ourselves, believing that we together shall have the same kingdom conferred upon us, and shall reign with Christ for ever and ever.

An old divine calls Mary Magdalene *apostola apostolorum,* that is, the apostle to the apostles. An apostle is one who is sent, and Mary Magdalene was sent to those whom Christ afterwards sent to the ends of the earth. In like manner, a poor humble woman may be an apostle to one who shall afterwards be a great divine. Let us hear, then, what this great apostle to the apostles has to say to us. She does not now tell us that Jesus Christ is about to ascend, she tells us that he has ascended; and whenever we draw around the table of our Lord, let us derive sweet influence from the fact that Jesus Christ has ascended. He ascended as a Conqueror, leading captivity captive. He ascended as a Forerunner for us, entering within the veil. He has ascended to make preparation for his people, according to his promise, 'I go to prepare a place for you. And if I go and prepare a place for you, I will come again, and receive you unto myself; that where I am, there ye may be also.' He has ascended as our Intercessor; there he stands for ever interceding before the throne of God for us, his children, his friends, his brethren. Oh, that we may now put our unfeigned and constant trust in him who died, putting equal trust in him who rose again, making this our glory, both in his dying and in his rising, that he hath ascended up on high, and taken his lawful place at the right hand of God, where he also maketh intercession for us!

Oh, that those who are dead in sin were quickened by God's Spirit, that they might know something of the preciousness of having a Father in heaven, the same Father that Jesus Christ had! Sinner, I pray the Lord to teach thee to believe in Jesus Christ; and if thou hast sinned with Mary Magdalene, may he help thee to believe with her, that thou mayest share in her sweet manifestations, and have a gracious message like hers to tell someday to the rest of thy brethren!

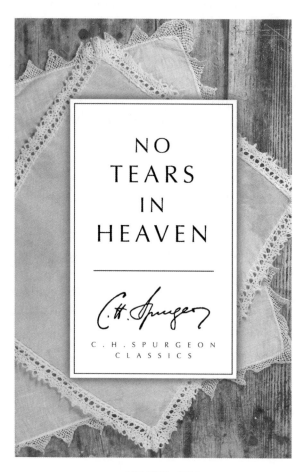

NO
TEARS
IN
HEAVEN

C . H . S P U R G E O N
C L A S S I C S

ISBN 978-78191-404-5

No Tears in Heaven

C.H. Spurgeon

'No Tears in Heaven' speaks of the great joy of the Christian faith – Heaven. The writings of Spurgeon, in his typically beautiful and penetrating style, will deepen our anticipation of Heaven and challenge us to a closer walk with God.

C.H SPURGEON, the great Victorian preacher, was a one of the most influential people of the second half of the 19th Century. He is known as the 'Prince of Preachers'. His sermons drew thousands to his church and he became a leading campaigner against liberal theology. Yet, at the heart of his desire to preach was a fierce love of people, a desire that meant that he did not neglect his pastoral ministry.

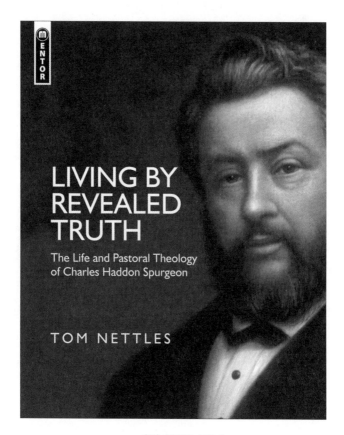

LIVING BY REVEALED TRUTH

The Life and Pastoral Theology
of Charles Haddon Spurgeon

TOM NETTLES

ISBN 978-78191-122-8

Living by Revealed Truth

The Life and Pastoral Theology of Charles Haddon Spurgeon

TOM NETTLES

Tom Nettles has spent more than fifteen years working on this magesterial biography of Charles Haddon Spurgeon, the famous nineteenth century preacher and writer. More than merely a biography it covers his life, ministry and also provides an indepth survey of his theology.

Charles Spurgeon is a mountain – a massive figure on the evangelical landscape. Tom Nettles now helps us to understand Charles Haddon Spurgeon as a man, a theologian, and one of the most influential pastors in church history. Nettles takes us into the heart of Charles Spurgeon's conviction and his pastoral theology. This is a book that will encourage, educate, and bless its readers.

R. Albert Mohler
President, The Southern Baptist Theological Seminary
Louisville, Kentucky

Tom Nettles' work now makes a major contribution to this growing appreciation of the man and his ministry. Mining neglected but important sources, he has given sharper definition to our picture of Spurgeon and produced a highly stimulating and readable account.

Michael Reeves
Theologian at Large, Wales Evangelical School of Theology
Bridgend, Wales

Thomas J. Nettles is Professor of Historical Theology at The Southern Baptist Theological Seminary in Louisville, Kentucky.

Christian Focus Publications

Our mission statement –

STAYING FAITHFUL

In dependence upon God we seek to impact the world through literature faithful to His infallible Word, the Bible. Our aim is to ensure that the Lord Jesus Christ is presented as the only hope to obtain forgiveness of sin, live a useful life and look forward to heaven with Him.

Our books are published in four imprints:

CHRISTIAN FOCUS

Popular works including biographies, commentaries, basic doctrine and Christian living.

CHRISTIAN HERITAGE

Books representing some of the best material from the rich heritage of the church.

MENTOR

Books written at a level suitable for Bible College and seminary students, pastors, and other serious readers. The imprint includes commentaries, doctrinal studies, examination of current issues and church history.

CF4•K

Children's books for quality Bible teaching and for all age groups: Sunday school curriculum, puzzle and activity books; personal and family devotional titles, biographies and inspirational stories – because you are never too young to know Jesus!

Christian Focus Publications Ltd,
Geanies House, Fearn, Ross-shire,
IV20 1TW, Scotland, United Kingdom.
www.christianfocus.com